HOW SHAKESPEARE WON THE WEST

I0139508

Richard Nelson

BROADWAY PLAY PUBLISHING INC
New York
www.broadwayplaypublishing.com
info@broadwayplaypublishing.com

HOW SHAKESPEARE WON THE WEST
©2010 by Richard Nelson

Cover photo by T Charles Erickson
First printing: September 2010
I S B N: 978-0-88145-452-9
Book design: Marie Donovan
Typography/page layout: Adobe InDesign
Typeface: Palatino Linotype

HOW SHAKESPEARE WON THE WEST was first produced by The Huntington Theater Company (Peter DuBois, Artistic Director, Michael Maso, Managing Director) on 5 September 2008. The cast and creative contributors were:

THOMAS JEFFERSON CALHOUN .... Will LeBow
ALICE CALHOUN...................................... Mary Beth Fisher
SUSAN CALHOUN.. Sarah Nealis
BUCK BUCHANAN..................................... Erik Lochtefeld
HANK DALEY ....Chris Henry Coffey
KATE DENIM ....Susannah Schulman
EDWARD OLDFIELD .... Jeremiah Kissel
RUTH OLDFIELD .... Kelly Hutchinson
JOHN GOUGH ....Joe Tapper
GEORGE DEMEREST...Jon De Vries
GEORGE EDGAR RICE................................... Ron Campbell
Ensemble ....Nicholas Combs & Curt Klump

other roles played by the company

Director... Jonathan Moscone
Scenic design...Antje Ellermann
Costume design................................... Laurie Churba Kohn
Lighting design .... Japhy Weideman
Music & sound design .....Rob Milburn & Michael Bodeen
Stage management .... Bethany Ford, Leslie Sears

CHARACTERS & SETTING

THOMAS JEFFERSON CALHOUN, *owner of the Bard Tavern, New York City, fifties. [also doubles as* FATHER ON THE PRAIRIE]

ALICE, THOMAS'*s wife, former actress, fifties*

SUSAN, *their daughter, early twenties [also doubles as* ELLEN BATEMAN]

BUCK BUCHANAN, *aspiring actor from Ohio, twenties*

HANK DALEY, *star actor, thirties or forites [also doubles as* MAN IN BUCKSKIN]

KATE DENIM, HANK'*s wife, a leading actress, thirties [also doubles as* KATE BATEMAN *&* MOTHER ON THE PRAIRIE]

GEORGE DEMEREST, *actor, forties or fifties [also doubles as* THIRD MINER, THIRD ACTOR, MINER WHO LOVES LEATHER]

EDWARD OLDFIELD, *actor, forties [also doubles as* SECOND MINER, SECOND ACTOR]

RUTH OLDFIELD, *thirties [also doubles as* LAURA AGNES]

JOHN GOUGH, *actor, twenties [also doubles as* FIRST MINER, FIRST ACTOR]

GEORGE EDGAR RICE, *impresario [also doubles as* BARNUM, BUFFALO BILL, *and* ABE *a lawyer in love with theater,* INTOLERANT MAN WITH ROPE, INDIAN CHIEF]

Other parts played by the company.

Role in THE THOMAS JEFFERSON CALHOUN STAR TROUPE:

Star.. HANK DALEY
Ingénue .... KATE DENIM (*later*: SUSAN)
Leading Actor .... THOMAS JEFFERSON CALHOUN
Leading Actress..ALICE CALHOUN
Juvenile .... BUCK BUCHANAN
Character Actor......................................GEORGE DEMEREST
Comic .... JOHN GOUGH
Utility Actor ....EDWARD OLDFIELD
Utility Actress .... RUTH OLDFIELD

New York City, and then across America and the West, 1848-1849.

The play should be performed without an intermission.

The following is based on real events.

to Susan Cumings

(GEORGE EDGAR RICE *speaks to us. He is lit by footlight.*)

RICE: 1848. Gold is discovered at Sutter's Mill, California. And gold fever sweeps the land. A quarter of a million people trek across the vast American continent creating everywhere new towns, and cities, and states. A quarter of a million picks and shovels and panning plates. A quarter of a million people asleep each night thousands of miles from home.
 Our story begins back East in a tavern...

(*Lights up on a tavern, a few customers [actors] sit around, drinking, playing cards.* THOMAS, ALICE *and their daughter* SUSAN *serve them. They speak to us as well.*)

RICE: —known by virtue of its clientele as—The Actors' Tavern.

THOMAS: But in truth licensed as— "The Bard".

RICE: We're on the corner of Park and Church Streets, New York City.

THOMAS: That's just around the corner from the Lyceum.

CUSTOMER: Where *Julius Caesar* is being given a rousing production with a fully staged battle.

ALICE: Down the street's The Bowery with Charles Kean's *Henry The Eighth*.

THOMAS: And Barnum's American Museum and Lecture Room.

SUSAN: Featuring this week: Major Little Finger—smaller than Tom Thumb, weighing thirteen pounds and standing but twenty-four inches tall!

ALICE: Across is the New Room where there's a combination of attractions: Chemistry, Magic. Diaphanous Tableaux.

CUSTOMER: And French plays.

THOMAS: Next door is the famed Broadway and the great Edwin Forrest's tragic Indian Chief, Metamora.

ALICE: And there's the City with the extraordinary Bateman Sisters, aged eleven and nine, continuing in their tribute to Shakespeare's greatest tragic roles.

RICE: All a mere stone's throw away from—The Bard. Whose owner—

THOMAS: *(Introducing himself to us:)* Thomas Jefferson Calhoun. Originally from New Haven, Connecticut.

RICE: As a young man dreamed of one day owning, not a tavern, but—

THOMAS: A stage.

RICE: Upon which he might star in both classical and contemporary plays.

THOMAS: My dream carried me to New York.

RICE: As great fires attract the moths.

THOMAS: Where I gained the rank of utility actor, a rank I happily wore for nearly a decade. And would have held for decades more.

RICE: The smell of theater being a perfume to some, a drug to many more.

THOMAS: Had I not met—.

ALICE: *(Introducing herself to us)* Alice. Then of the rank of ingénue, but with, it being generally forecast, a future as leading woman, if not actually, star.

THOMAS: So I abandoned my cherished profession to provide for my wife. Took a job in the very tavern I'd so often frequented before, and which through diligence and hard work, in time, I came to own.

RICE: In the meantime, Alice woke up one day to discover—

ALICE: I was no longer an ingénue, but not yet a leading woman either.

RICE: She was in that actresses' netherworld twixt work—

ALICE: And work.

RICE: And like so many others before and since—

ALICE: I vowed—

THOMAS: With my full backing—

ALICE: To wait it out.

RICE: But instead—

SUSAN: *(Introducing herself)* Became pregnant with me.

RICE: And never acted upon a stage again.

ALICE: And never regretted it.

THOMAS: Me neither. Not once. Not for a single second.

RICE: Until one cold wet October day, in 1848, when—

(BUCK BUCHANAN *is at the doorway to the bar. All stop and look at him—a stranger. He slowly walks in.)*

RICE: —a man named Buck Buchanan arrived with a story to tell.

(BUCK *is suddenly in the middle of his story, and the* CALHOUNS *and the customers, excited, are shouting at him,* "I don't believe you!" "That doesn't make sense!" "He's pulling our leg." etc.)

RICE: Let him talk! Be quiet! Let him speak!

(The others quiet down. BUCK *continues:)*

BUCK: I tell you it's true. It's what's happening out there, I swear on my dead mother's grave! The miners out there in California—they're not who you'd think they'd be.

CUSTOMER: So who are they?!

BUCK: I'm trying to tell you! Will you shut up! The miners are pretty well educated for one. So it makes sense. They're standing all day, up to their waists in water, panning. Their minds drift. They get talking to each other. So what do they talk about? This is what I'm trying to tell you.

(Lights up on three MINERS *"waist-deep in water", panning. those in the tavern turn to watch them—as this is* BUCK's *story. After a moment:)*

FIRST MINER: Well, you got it yet? *(Spits)*

SECOND MINER: I'm thinking. *(He thinks, then repeats the question:)* "If...music...be the...food...of love"??

FIRST MINER: *(To the* THIRD MINER:*)* He doesn't know it! *(Laughs)*

THIRD MINER: Give him a chance. Come on, Starks, I got a sawbuck on you.

SECOND MINER: "If music..."

FIRST MINER: "...be the food of love..." *(Short pause, then:)* Time's up!

THIRD MINER: *(Yelling at the* FIRST MINER:*)* "Play on!! Give me excess of it, surfeiting the appetite may sicken and so die!"

FIRST MINER: *(Laughing and taking the* THIRD MINER's *sawbuck)* He doesn't know his Shakespeare!!

(Lights off the MINERS; *we are back in the tavern. Silence)*

THOMAS: *(Finally, to* BUCK:*)* You—actually saw this happen? They're standing in the goddamn creek and talking about—?

BUCK: Shakespeare. I said I heard about it. I told you I haven't been to California myself—. From actors passing back through Ohio. I'm from Ohio. They showed me their pouches stuffed with gold.

ALICE: The actors had gold?? How did actors get gold?

RICE: He's getting to that. Sh-sh.

(They turned to RICE, *now back to* BUCK:*)*

BUCK: Of course, it was pure luck that the actors were in California when gold was discovered.

(Lights up on three ACTORS *[the same who played the* MINERS*]. The customers and the* CALHOUNS *turn and watch the* ACTORS.*)*

BUCK: And at first they thought they'd give up the acting and just start to dig. But then—one of them had another idea...

FIRST ACTOR: *(To the other two* ACTORS*)* All these men who are coming out here?

BUCK: He said one night to the others around their campfire.

FIRST ACTOR: These lonely miners, I've noticed have nothing to do with their evenings. So—they just drink, they whore, they get into a lot of trouble. Maybe...

BUCK: His voice dropped.

FIRST ACTOR: They'd pay to see—a...play.

BUCK: *(Repeats with emphasis to the Tavern:)* To— see—a—play.

ALICE: What sort of play?

BUCK: That's just what they went about discussing.

(FIRST ACTOR *to the other two* ACTORS, *as the tavern watches with great interest:*)

FIRST ACTOR: Let's name our choices. One: there's the second act of the *Double-Bedded Room*.

SECOND ACTOR: I have nothing to play in that.

FIRST ACTOR: I think it is one of the funniest pieces of theater written in the last ten years. And if I were a miner and I'd spent my day—.

SECOND ACTOR: You've got the biggest part in that!

FIRST ACTOR: Two: *Richelieu*.

(FIRST ACTOR *pauses. The other two just stare at him.*)

FIRST ACTOR: What?? Anyone want to comment? Either for or... Anyone not in favor of *Richelieu*? Then if no one's opposed to—. (*He starts to write this down.*)

THIRD ACTOR: We didn't say—.

SECOND ACTOR: (*Same time:*) Don't write that down!

FIRST ACTOR: I think I'm a damn good Richelieu!! Three...

BUCK: (*To the tavern and us:*) The actors went through their lists of plays, discarding this one, then—that one. And so it might have continued throughout the night had not a voice interrupted:

VOICE: *King Lear.*

BUCK: Said a gentleman...

(*Lights up on a man in buckskin.*)

BUCK: ...in buckskin.

(*The* ACTORS *are startled, and turn toward the man. Those in the tavern watch with great interest.*)

FIRST ACTOR: Excuse me?

SECOND ACTOR: Are you speaking to us?

MAN: *King Lear*—is what they'd like to see.

THIRD ACTOR: *The King Lear* by William Shakespeare?

MAN: That's the one. Know it?

SECOND ACTOR: Of course we—. We're actors!

MAN: So how much will it take for you actors to put it on? Will this be enough?

(The MAN tosses a small bag at the ACTORS' feet. They gasp. Lights out on the ACTORS, we are back in the tavern:)

BUCK: And the dust in that pouch had to be worth— well hundreds of dollars.

(Short pause as they all digest this. Then:)

THOMAS: So they put on...?

BUCK: What do you think?

ALICE: Did they know *King Lear*? The actors.

BUCK: Enough of it.

SUSAN: Where did they play?

BUCK: I've heard there are trees out West—you cut them down—and their stumps are wide enough to perform an entire play on.

SUSAN: Oh God!

BUCK: But in this instance—they didn't play upon the stumps of giant primeval trees, but rather, they built themselves a stage in the backroom of a local saloon.

(Lights up on a curtain. We are backstage in this little makeshift theater that BUCK describes. The three ACTORS are preparing for the play. Those in the tavern turn and watch.)

BUCK: They took old doors, laid them out across chairs—this would be their stage floor. Candles were stuck into empty bottles and lit.

(Through the curtain: the light from these candles.)

SUSAN: *(Excited:)* As—footlights!

BUCK: Correct. And that night miners began arriving from miles and miles around...

(Noise of a crowd growing behind the curtain.)

BUCK: ...paying in gold mostly for a seat, any seat, or a place on a bench or even a plot of air to stand in.

(Noise grows.)

BUCK: Elbow to elbow, cheek by jowl, they sat waiting for the show to begin!

(A rousing version of Arkansas Traveler on banjo is heard through the curtain. The audience is starting to clap along with it, whooping and hollering.)

(Then the THIRD ACTOR, after taking a deep breath, goes through the curtain and onto "the stage." Sudden silence from the crowd)

(Then from "the stage" we hear:)

THIRD ACTOR: *(Voice, as Lear)* Give me the map there. Know that we have divided in three our kingdom. and 'tis our intent—.

VOICE: *(From the audience) Fast* intent!

THIRD ACTOR: *(Voice, confused;)* What???

VOICES: *(Entire audience) Fast* intent!!

SECOND ACTOR: *(Watching what is happening, to the* FIRST ACTOR*:)* They're correcting him.

THIRD ACTOR: *(Voice, continuing, but shaken now:)* Conferring them...them... *(He has forgotten the lines, opens the curtain and whispers desperately to the other* ACTORS*:)* What's the line?

VOICES: *(Entire audience) To shake all cares and business from our age!!!*

BUCK: *(To the tavern and us;)* They—knew the whole play. Every damn word.

(We are suddenly half-way through the play:)

VOICES: *(Entire audience)* Now gods stand up for bastards!! Yahoo!!!

BUCK: Right down to—

VOICES: *(Entire audience, in a big stage whisper:)* Pray, undo this button.

(And sudden silence. The three ACTORS come back through the curtain, not sure what they have just experienced or what awaits them when from the stage: a huge and thunderous cheer. The ACTORS look at each other and go back "on stage" for their bows.)

BUCK: One of the actors told me...

(SECOND ACTOR, dazed, comes back through the curtain and speaks to the tavern and us:)

SECOND ACTOR: Their ovation was a force of nature, a hurricane, a duster, a thousand thunderclaps.

(FIRST and THIRD ACTORS come back out, carrying pouches of gold. They too can't believe what has just happened. They now speak to the tavern and to us.)

FIRST ACTOR: And when we were finally allowed to leave the stage—.

THIRD ACTOR: We could barely carry off all the sacks of gold and dust that had been thrown at our feet.

(They hold out the gold for us to see. From the other side of the curtain the crowd continues to cheer and chant.)

SECOND ACTOR: And upon discovering that we were leaving town that night—.

FIRST ACTOR: We'd assumed the worst.

SECOND ACTOR: The planks of our stage were ripped up and used as litters, to carry us to the edge of town.

THIRD ACTOR: Where we at last were bid a warm farewell...

FIRST ACTOR: And as we departed upon our journey, we were serenaded with tunes performed in rounds and rich harmonies. These, we realized, had been worked out and rehearsed by the miners in their endless and lonely hours looking for gold.

SECOND ACTOR: And the songs they sang? They were from the plays of Shakespeare.

(From behind the curtain we hear the crowd singing a Shakespearean song.)

CROWD: *(Singing:)* With hey-ho, the wind and the rain...

(Lights fade on the stunned group in the tavern and on the backstage and the three ACTORS with their sacks of gold.)

RICE: *(Singing, to us:)* With hey-ho, the wind and the rain. *(Then:)* Later that evening, Thomas and Alice tried to find a moment to speak in private...

(Evening now, and THOMAS and ALICE are cleaning up the tavern. BUCK, with his guitar, is trying to teach SUSAN the song:)

BUCK: *(Strumming:)* The rain it raineth every day..

ALICE: Do you have to do that here?

SUSAN: Buck's just—.

ALICE: I know what Buck is just... We need to clean up. You're in the way.

SUSAN: Do you want me to help?

ALICE & THOMAS: No!

SUSAN: Come on, Buck. We're in the way here...

(They go. Soon from off we hear BUCK continuing to teach SUSAN chords on the guitar.)

ALICE: Thomas—

THOMAS: *(Same time:)* Alice—

(They stop, then:)

THOMAS: You first.

(ALICE hesitates, looks off, then:)

ALICE: Thomas, I miss acting. I miss the theater. I miss performing in front of people. And I have missed it every day since I stopped. I wake up some nights feeling that something has been removed from inside me.

THOMAS: Why have you never told me this before? That young man's story has got you excited.

ALICE: We've heard other stories. We know that people are going West.

THOMAS: Miners. Prospectors. I'm too old to—.

ALICE: And actors. We've heard of actors.

THOMAS: Is that what you want?

(ALICE looks at THOMAS. Then:)

ALICE: I'm sorry.

THOMAS: And the tavern?

(ALICE shrugs.)

THOMAS: Sell it? And buy a wagon? Supplies? Costumes?

ALICE: Yes, costumes!

THOMAS: And our daughter?

ALICE: She's not too young.

THOMAS: Isn't she?

ALICE: How old was I when I arrived here? *(Short pause)* I know what a shock this must be to you.

THOMAS: So—to put together an acting troupe, we'd need—a utility female, a utility male. That's what I used to be—.

ALICE: Thomas, it'll be our wagon. *(Then realizing:)*

THOMAS: *(Points to her:)* Leading lady. *(To himself:)* Leading man.

ALICE: That's us.

THOMAS: An ingénue. Susan?

ALICE: She hasn't any experience.

THOMAS: I have been teaching her for months.

ALICE: I thought we'd agreed not to encourage her acting.

THOMAS: And she tells me you've been teaching her too. And there's the juvenile. This Buck?

ALICE: If he'll come with us.

THOMAS: He will. I've spoken to him.

ALICE: You what??

THOMAS: I've felt something's been missing for a long time too, Alice. I was going to say those same things to you.

ALICE: Oh, Thomas!

(ALICE hugs THOMAS.)

THOMAS: Can we trust this man?

ALICE: *(Hugging him)* It'll be our wagon.

THOMAS: *(Pulling back:)* You know—it's not going to be easy. I mean—we're changing our whole lives—like that. *(Snaps his fingers)*

ALICE: Or is it that we're finding our lives again?

(BUCK and SUSAN have returned and stand at a distance. THOMAS sees them, and pulls away from ALICE:)

THOMAS: She's agreed to go!

(SUSAN and BUCK react—excited. SUSAN runs to hug her mother. ALICE is confused:)

ALICE: It was my idea! I'm the one who—.

(But the others aren't listening:)

THOMAS: So who else do we need, Buck?

(BUCK has a small pad in hand:)

BUCK: Leading male, leading—

THOMAS: That's us.

SUSAN: But I thought you used to—.

THOMAS: *(Smiling:)* Not anymore. *(He takes ALICE's hand.)*

BUCK: Then—we need—the utilities?

(THOMAS nods.)

BUCK: And a character man, a comic—and a star.

ALICE: Star!?

SUSAN: We can't go without a star. But where are we going to find one of them?

(Short pause. No one knows.)

ALICE: And if we don't find one?

(They turn to THOMAS.)

THOMAS: Then—I don't think we can go.

ALICE: So—let's find a star!!!

(Others react with excitement, and determination.)

SUSAN: *(To us:)* We drew up a long list of possible stars.

(THOMAS is writing in a small notebook.)

THOMAS: So this is everyone we can think of. I have put the names in order—and drawn a line here. *(He shows them.)* Anyone below this line—well, I don't think they

can do it. For my money, I don't think it's even worth
doing with one of them. As star. Agree? Do we all
agree?

(They agree.)

THOMAS: I mean, you might as well just...

SUSAN: *(To us)* A week later father drew another line.

ALICE: *(Pointing to someone low on the list:)* He's not bad.
Why was he so low?

THOMAS: She's right. He's not bad at all. And he's
not that old. He looks a lot younger on stage than in
person. He pulls it off somehow. Good for him. I think
he's a lot better actor than he's been given credit for. I
think—.

SUSAN: He's dead.

THOMAS: What??

SUSAN: I heard this week he'd died. Of old age.

(Short pause, as they collect themselves, then:)

THOMAS: Well, I for one am not discouraged. I hope
none of you are so easily discouraged. You know—
who needs a star? Maybe we don't even need one.
Maybe—I could be the star.

(They all just stare at him, then:)

RICE: And then—perhaps under the category of "Will
Wonders Never Cease" —in walked:

*(HANK DALEY, handsome and drunk, enters the Bard,
supported by two friends/ACTORS.)*

(The others stare at him, he stares back, then:)

HANK: Is this the...? *(He blinks, looking around.)*

THOMAS: *(Being helpful)* The Bard, Mister Daley. *(To the
others:)* Hank Daley!

FIRST FRIEND: He's been drinking for six hours.

SECOND FRIEND: He got fired, didn't you hear?

BUCK: *(To the others:)* Who's Hank—?

ALICE: Hank Daley got fired?!

FIRST FRIEND: Hackett fired him.

ALICE: Daley is Hackett's star.

BUCK: His star??? *(To others:)* His star!!

HANK: *(To everyone:)* Do you know when I was first upon the stage, friends? Does anyone care to know? I will tell you... *(He turns to* SUSAN.*)* Do you know the play— *(Tries to remember, then remembers:) peter white*? You know the little rag doll in it? That he's always... When I was six months old? I played that rag doll. Right out of my mother's arms and onto the... You should have heard the round I got on my exit. I can still hear it. I remember it... *(He has sat down, and now puts his head on the table.)*

THOMAS: *(In a half-whisper)* He's been with Hackett for years. He'd never fire him.

SECOND FRIEND: He was caught with Hackett's wife.

THOMAS: But I've seen Hackett's wife.

HANK: *(Head on table)* I kept my eyes closed.

BUCK: This Daley, he's good?

THOMAS: The next Edwin Forrest people are always saying.

ALICE: I never actually heard anyone say that.

HANK: *(Head on table)* I say it.

SUSAN: He's got such a beautiful wife, why would he—?

FIRST FRIEND: Hackett wouldn't give me a raise. So it was to get even.

BUCK: *(To the others:)* So—*he's* fired.

SECOND FRIEND: And blackballed. People are saying we won't see Hank Daley on any stage in this town for years and years.

FIRST FRIEND: He's been drinking all day. Too scared to go home.

(THOMAS, BUCK, ALICE and SUSAN look at each other, then:)

THOMAS: Well...let's ask him.

(They approach HANK who suddenly lifts his head, startling them and begins Jacques' Seven Ages of Man speech.)

HANK: "At first, the infant,
Mewling and puking in the nurse's arms.
Then the whining schoolboy, with his..."
And so forth, and so forth and forth. Until...
"Sans teeth.
Sans eyes.
Sans..."

(And HANK passes out, his head hits the table.)

(Pause. They look at him.)

RICE: *(To us:)* And so—they found their star. Next came George Demerest, character actor.

(Part of the stage now represents the City Theater. GEORGE DEMEREST explains:)

GEORGE: *(To us)* Presently performing at the City with the—beautiful Bateman Sisters aged nine and eleven in their sensational show and big hit—*The Greatest Scenes From Shakespeare.*

(ELLEN, age nine, enters as Richard II, hump and all.)

ELLEN: *(In a loud squeaky kid's voice:)*
"Now is the Winter of our discontent..."
(She is one's worst nightmare of a child performer, all show, all pleasing, even as Richard III)

GEORGE: *(To us;)* Ellen, the younger, was deemed by all—the most versatile.

(ELLEN suddenly whirls around, pulls out her hump and becomes Hamlet.)

ELLEN: "Oh what a rogue and peasant slave am I..."

GEORGE: Her Shylock was particularly...what is the word?

(ELLEN has suddenly stuck on a big fake nose and beard, appearing both anti-semitic and unattractive, while continuing to mug:)

ELLEN: "If you prick us, do we not bleed?
(She pretends to prick herself and cackles.)
If you tickle us, do we not laugh?
(Tickles herself and cackles.)
If you poison us, do we not die?"

GEORGE: Unfortunately not. Kate, the older, and favorite with the critics, was the more physically becoming, but less accomplished one.

(KATE has entered, now as Portia in a short tunic, showing a lot of leg, and perhaps—even a little thigh?)

KATE: "The quality of mercy
(Gesture)
is not strained;
(Gesture)
It droppeth *(Gesture)* as the gentle rain from heaven
(Gesture)
Upon—the place beneath."
(Gestures, gives a big sexy smile to the audience, and perhaps shows a little more thigh.)

GEORGE: And George Demerest played the parts that were left.

(ELLEN has suddenly turned herself into King Lear, with KATE as the dead Cordelia whom she drags along.)

GEORGE: "Is this the promised end?"

ELLEN: *(As Lear)*
"No, no, no life?
Why should a dog, a horse, a rat have life,
And thou no breath at all? Thou'lt come no more,
Never!"
(Weeps)
"Please, you—undo this button."

(ELLEN has turned to GEORGE who leans over to undo a button, but has trouble because the button's so small. She grows impatient.)

ELLEN: Undo it!!!

(KATE opens her eyes to watch.)

GEORGE: *(In a panic:)* My hands are too big. The button's so small!

(GEORGE tries again, then KATE jumps up, undoes her sister's button, and goes back to being dead.)

(ELLEN/Lear dies. And thunderous applause, cheers from the audience, which the girls acknowledge, even the "dead" one. And the lights fade out on the City Theater and we are back in the Bard.)

(GEORGE stands there, the others looking at him.)

GEORGE: Where do I sign?

(THOMAS hands GEORGE a pen and gives him the contract.)

GEORGE: Can I ask something?

(The others nod.)

GEORGE: Will there be any performing—children in the troupe?

(The others look at each other and then shake their heads: "No. No.")

(As GEORGE signs)

THOMAS: Don't you want to ask anything else?

GEORGE: No. I only had that one question. *(He signs.)*

*(*HANK, *still with head on table, turns to* ALICE *and* SUSAN.)*

HANK: So—you got George Demerest.

ALICE: You know him?

HANK: I do. A good, kind man. Quiet. Sensitive. Full of dignity. So rare in an actor.

RICE: *(To us)* And then came the Oldfields, the utility players.

(The OLDFIELDS *enter.)*

RUTH: *(To us)* Ruth.

EDWARD: *(To us)* Edward.

(We are suddenly in the middle of a conversation between the OLDFIELDS *and* THOMAS, ALICE, BUCK *and* SUSAN.)*

*(*GEORGE *sits with* HANK *watching from a distance.)*

(A burst of laughter, then:)

ALICE: Where did you say you were from?

EDWARD: Summersets.

RUTH: It's near Brighton.

EDWARD: Quite a fashionable part of England, the North.

(The OLDFIELDS *speak in very bad fake British accents.)*

RUTH: Have you ever been...?

ALICE: No. No.

EDWARD: I can't tell you how very taken we are with your stories, Buck, of the—do you call it the *Wild* West? Or have I just coined that?

ALICE: I think I've heard it.

EDWARD: You see how new everything is to us, old chaps. Life lived in a castle is terribly—spoiling.

THOMAS: I can imagine.

RUTH: My husband was saying—this might amuse you— *(She laughs.)* —that after a season at the Dreary Lane Playhouse Theatre anything with ventilation would seem wild!

(EDWARD and ALICE laugh.)

BUCK: You played the—? Isn't it called the—?

EDWARD: *(dramatically)* Argos thymos era tempta!

BUCK: What's that?

RUTH: It's what's inscribed above its golden doors.

ALICE: What does it mean?

EDWARD: "Watch your back!" *(He laughs.)* An English theatre joke. The English theatre—there's nothing like it. *(Turns to RUTH)* Is there, Ducky? *(To THOMAS)* So where do we sign?

(THOMAS points to the contracts on the table in front of them. As they sign:)

GEORGE: *(To HANK)* They're not English, are they?

(HANK, still head on table, shakes his head.)

GEORGE: And—I'm just guessing now—but she's not his wife.

HANK: No.

GEORGE: You know them?

HANK: I do.

GEORGE: She's—what? His sister?

HANK: That is correct.

GEORGE: I've never seen them before.

HANK: Not from here. From Upstate. Albany. It's where I know them from. But I didn't even know she acted. In Albany—she was just a whore.

(At the other table, RUTH has whispered something to THOMAS, who bursts out laughing.)

RICE: Finding the right comic proved to be—tricky.

BUCK: *(To us)* Every theater, every amusement—.

(They all speak to us:)

THOMAS: The circus, every backwater—

ALICE: Such as Pesh's Walhalla on Canal with its Ethiopian Mountain singers.

SUSAN: And English female acrobats—

BUCK: Was scoured without—success.

ALICE: No comic, in all the city, it appeared, was willing to go West.

BUCK: So Buck offered to play the comic roles.

ALICE: And they kept looking—harder.

SUSAN: Then one afternoon in the middle of Indian Summer, Susan happened to take a walk and turn down Orange Street.

THOMAS: When she was startled to hear a familiar voice—.

ALICE: Coming from an open window—.

BUCK: Of a church.

(JOHN GOUGH appears, standing on a chair, "the pulpit" of a church.)

JOHN: *(To us)* Where John Gough, dressed—sort of—as a minister, stands in a pulpit— *(Gestures—the chair)* —addressing an unseen, and very bored congregation. *(He turns to the "congregation" and tries to read from notes.)* So—the Bible Says... *(Looks up to the congregation:)* Sorry, I'm having a hard time reading Reverend Winthrop's handwriting.

(SUSAN, *on Orange Street, looks up at* JOHN *and recognizes him.)*

SUSAN: *(To us and the others in the tavern who are watching:)* It's—John Gough!

JOHN: *(To the congregation)* I think I've got it now. The Reverend really needs to work on his handwriting. *(Reads:)* "So—the Bible says..." *(He stops again, ponders, to himself:)* That doesn't make any sense.

(JOHN *happens to look out the "window" and sees:)*

JOHN: Susan??!

(SUSAN *waves,* JOHN *puts his finger to his lips and continues:)*

JOHN: Here's something—I can read. A list supplied by Reverend Winthrop of moral improvements not specifically addressed in the Bible. Cold Showers, for both men and women. Loose clothing. For men— especially the trousers.

ALICE: *(To us:)* John Gough and Susan had grown up together.

THOMAS: *(To us)* He began working at the Bard when he was twelve.

ALICE: He used to do things.

THOMAS: Silly things.

ALICE: With napkins or bottles or a tray of empty glasses.

SUSAN: *(To us)* That always made me laugh.

ALICE: Susan waited for him on the church steps.

(JOHN *"comes out" of the church and* SUSAN *grabs him.)*

SUSAN: So you're a minister! I didn't know.

JOHN: Yes, a minister. But just for the day, it's—. The normal one wanted a day off, and he'd seen me play a minister in *The Witch Of Windermere*. You didn't happen to see me in—?

SUSAN: No. No, I'm sorry. You seemed very good. *(She gestures toward the church.)*

JOHN: I wanted to have it memorized but—.

SUSAN: You seemed very—good.

JOHN: Did I? It's the most lines I've had in... God, look how old you are.

SUSAN: It's only been a year, John. Why did you run away? Why didn't you ever come back and see us?

ALICE: And she took his arm in hers, and as they walked together down Orange, he told her his story.

(All in The Bard watch and listen:)

JOHN: I was offered a job. By P T Barnum no less. He'd sent a letter to your father's tavern. Addressed to me! I said to myself—here's the chance you've been praying for, John Gough. So I left. I quit. Of course your father's advice was—.

THOMAS: See if it's a good job first, John.

JOHN: But I knew better. Oh did I. And laughed in his face. *(He laughs at THOMAS, then:)* Then that afternoon I went to see Mister Barnum.

(RICE dressed as P T BARNUM stands in his office, JOHN "enters".)

(All, including SUSAN, watch.)

BARNUM: Good of you to come, young man. I'm sure you've a busy schedule.

JOHN: No, not at all.

BARNUM: So I won't keep you then.

JOHN: Had he even heard me? Was he listening?

BARNUM: Sit down, Mister Gough.

JOHN: There was nowhere to sit.

BARNUM: May we get you anything? No?

JOHN: He didn't even let me answer.

BARNUM: Let me get to the point then. I have a role I wish you to play. A role for which, from everything I've heard about you, son, you are uniquely qualified.

JOHN: Thank you, sir, for showing such... But he wasn't listening.

BARNUM: Do you know the Hippodrome?

JOHN: Of course I knew the Hippodrome.

SUSAN: Who doesn't know the Hippodrome?

BARNUM: Then you've noticed that they've opened a show of freaks! What right does the Hippodrome have in showing freaks?! And across the street from Barnums! Only I do freaks, Mister Gough! Only I!

JOHN: How dare they!!

BARNUM: I'm pleased you see the injustice. Here. I want you to take this.

(BARNUM *hands* JOHN *a jar.*)

JOHN: And then he handed me a jar of molasses.

SUSAN: Molasses?

JOHN: Mister Barnum explained.

BARNUM: I would like you to spread this molasses all over your body, Mister Gough.

SUSAN: What??

JOHN: He said, "I would like—"

SUSAN: I heard. I just didn't under—

BARNUM: Head to toe, Mister Gough.

JOHN: Why would I spread molasses all over me? I'm smiling now, thinking this must be a joke.

BARNUM: To attract flies and smells and animals of all sorts so as you stand by the box office of the Hippodrome you will drive *their* customers away.

SUSAN: *(Covers her mouth and laughs)* No!!

JOHN: Yes! So I stood in front of the box office of the Hippodrome covered in molasses for seven straight days.

SUSAN: Seven days?!

JOHN: Which is longer, I was told later—

BARNUM: Than anyone has ever done before! A couple of days more—

JOHN: I learned later—

BARNUM: And you, Mister Gough, would have qualified—.

JOHN: In Mister Barnum's eyes—

BARNUM: As a bonafide—freak!!

JOHN: I'm told—I should take that as a compliment.

SUSAN: *(Laughing:)* John Gough, you are the funniest man I have ever...

(Everyone in the tavern is laughing now at JOHN's story, then all including SUSAN have the same thought at the same time:)

SUSAN: Wait. What are you doing now, John?

(SUSAN takes JOHN by the arm, leads him to the others in the tavern.)

RICE: *(As he takes off the BARNUM coat, etc)* And so—they had their comic.

(Boistrous greetings and introductions, as JOHN meets all in the tavern.)

(ALICE *is handing out beers.*)

THOMAS: Quiet! Quiet!

(*They all quiet down.*)

THOMAS: So—that's it then. (*Pointing out:*) Comic. Juvenile. Ingénue. Character man, utilities. Leading actors. And—star. We're—a full company.

ALICE: (*Amazed:*) We are.

(*They all take this in.*)

BUCK: We can now go anytime.

ALICE: We can.

(*Short pause, as they take this in.*)

THOMAS: I just want to say that I don't think I could have dreamed of a better company than this.

(*Others agree, look around, smile.*)

(THOMAS *holds up a book:*)

THOMAS: *The Plays of William Shakespeare.* (*He opens it.*) Will we be worthy? (*He looks at the others:*) Of these great words? Of these characters? No, of these people! Living people are in here! (*The book*) As we are so small, and they—so great. Well, we'll have to do our best.

JOHN: And the name?

THOMAS: What??

GEORGE: We decided on a name.

THOMAS: No one asked me—.

RUTH: "The Thomas Jefferson Calhoun Star Troupe."

(THOMAS *is overwhelmed.*)

HANK: As you put up the money.

THOMAS: Before I start to cry—let's pack!

(*They turn to go and pack and for the first time see a woman,* KATE DENIM, *standing in the doorway.*)

HANK: *(Stunned, quietly:)* Kate.

BUCK: Who is—?

ALICE: *(Under her breath)* Kate Denim. Hank's wife.

THOMAS: *(To BUCK, in a whisper)* You've never seen her on the stage?

(BUCK shakes his head.)

SUSAN: I have seen her Ophelia ten times.

ALICE: Sh-sh.

HANK: What are you doing here, Kate?

(KATE looks around, then, smiling:)

KATE: So—this is The Bard. The younger girls come here, I think. I hear them in the dressing room talking about—coming here. After a show. How come you never brought me here?

ALICE: Miss Denim can I get you anything?

KATE: No, thank you. *(To HANK)* You never brought me to any places like this. *(She smiles.)* Somehow I think I got this reputation as someone—who wouldn't go to places like this. I don't know how that happened. I don't know what I did. Thank you for your letter. It was a lovely letter. You could always—write a letter.

GEORGE: Maybe we should leave them alone.

KATE: No! Please. I'd feel just awful if I ruined... You were—about to pack. So—these are the actors?

(HANK nods.)

KATE: How do you do? An attractive company. *(She looks at each one, smiles, then:)* As you see, I've brought my bag.

(For the first time, they all notice her suitcase.)

HANK: *(Confused:)* Kate???

KATE: I'd like to come with you.

EDWARD: What did she say??

KATE: May I? Would you consider it?

HANK: Kate?

KATE: I would like to come with all of you. Would that be possible?

HANK: I don't understand.

KATE: As I said—you write such wonderful letters.

HANK: Kate!!

(HANK *hugs* KATE.)

KATE: (*Hugging back:*) So you don't mind?

HANK: (*To the others:*) She forgives me!

(*As* HANK *and* KATE *continue to hug*)

THOMAS: (*To* ALICE) Think of it—Kate Denim with—us.

EDWARD: She's the best actress in New York.

GEORGE: How would you know? I thought you just got here from "Dreary Lane.'

EDWARD: That's true. But it's what I've heard.

SUSAN: (*Concerned:*) But what'll she play?

RUTH: The ingénue roles, of course! You couldn't ask for a better ingénue.

SUSAN: Oh. I see.

BUCK: Wait! What about Susan? We promised her those parts.

ALICE: Oh she won't mind! She understands. Kate Denim's a real actress. We'll find other things for Susan to do.

KATE: (*Still hugging* HANK, *not having heard this conversation:*) You know—I think I would now like to try a beer!

ALICE: Susan, get Miss Denim a beer.

(SUSAN *goes off.* BUCK *and* JOHN *watch her.*)

JOHN: *(To* BUCK:) Poor Susan.

BUCK: I know. I know.

KATE: *(Still with her arm around her husband:)* Thank you, everyone—for being so kind and understanding. I can't wait—to leave this city behind. And— *(She turns to* HANK.) —start all over again.

(SUSAN *returns with the beer.*)

SUSAN: Miss Denim. Your beer.

(KATE *takes the beer mug. She obviously has never held a beer mug before. She smells it, then takes a gulp and chokes, then:*)

KATE: I like it. It's good. I really do like it. *("Smiling" she tries another sip.)*

THOMAS: Well—as I was saying, let's pack!

JOHN: *(Stopping everyone;)* Wait!

(They look at JOHN. *He bows his head.)*

JOHN: May God guide us and protect us.

ALL: Amen.

(As they go off to pack:)

JOHN: *(To* GEORGE:) I played a minister in *The Witch Of Windermere.*

(As they gather their bags, BUCK *plays his guitar and sings* [Old Chisham Trail]:)

BUCK: *(Sings)*
Now come along boys
And listen to my tale
And I'll tell you about my troubles
On the ol' Chisolm Trail
Come a-ty-yi yippi
Yippi-a yippi-a

Come a-ty-yi-yippi
Yippi-a.
I started up the trail
October twenty-third
Left old texas
With a two-mile herd...

(Others join in, and their journey begins:)

ALL: Come a ty-yi-yippi
Yippi-a yippi-a
Come a-ty-yi-yippi
Yippi-a

JOHN: *(Shouts out:)* Yah-hoo!!!

ALL: For a ten-dollar horse
And a forty-dollar saddle
I'm a goin' punchin'
Them long-horned cattle
Come a-ty-yi-yippi
Yippi-a yippi-a
Come a-ty-yi-yippi
Yippi-a.
(They speak to us:)

EDWARD: The first leg of the journey!

RUTH: One thousand miles to the banks of the Missouri River!

JOHN: Past lush rolling hills. And deep blue lakes.

SUSAN: Meadows of purple flowers.

GEORGE: Birch tree forests. Then oak forests.

THOMAS: Then pine.

HANK: Over brooks with fish the size of nine-year-old girls.

ALICE: Come right to the bank, and with their fins, I'd swear they were waving hello.

BUCK: Black crows with voices so deep they could have played the opera.

(They are walking.)

THOMAS: *(In awe, and a bit intimidated)* Lovely,isn't it?

GEORGE: George Demerest turns out to be an excellent wagon driver.

JOHN: John Gough is handy with a tool.

BUCK: And Buck, they learn, was a wheelwright back home in Ohio.

ALICE: So we were in some pretty fair hands.

KATE: And Kate Denim.

GEORGE: Dear Kate Denim.

HANK: Sweet Kate.

KATE: Turns out to be a wonderful cook.

EDWARD: With a winning smile.

THOMAS: A warmth we all felt.

SUSAN: She touched the lives of all of us. Like an angel. Who could stay mad?

KATE: *(To SUSAN)* If you'd like, later I'll help you with any speech.

GEORGE: There was nothing this great actress was too grand for.

KATE: Mister Demerest, as I'm doing Hank's shirts, I might just as well be doing yours.

BUCK: She knew what was needed.

KATE: Men—what about a drink? I know what you're thinking—don't mind us ladies.

HANK: *(As he takes out his flask to have a drink)* And what we didn't need.

KATE: Except for my husband. (*She takes away his flask.*) Who'll have to settle for a kiss from me. (*She kisses him.*)

RUTH: And so on...

KATE: Ruth—lovely hair. And Alice, will you sit down and rest? And Edward, why wasn't I born with those eyelashes, they're beautiful.

SUSAN: Until—she'd become the fire, the flame, the hearth around which we were all drawn.

JOHN: She laughed at every joke.

(*KATE laughs.*)

GEORGE: Listened to the same story for the eighth time.

THOMAS: The one about the missed entrance.

ALICE: Broken prop.

GEORGE: Forgotten lines.

(*KATE laughs.*)

BUCK: And there was Hank, her husband, who soaked her up as a sun worshipper does the sun.

HANK: A happier, luckier man would be hard to find. My eyes never leaving my goddess, my shrine.

ALICE: We tried not to notice.

EDWARD: But we weren't blind.

THOMAS: And so the first one thousand miles passed—without incident.

BUCK: Except for one.

(*They stop walking. they are in front of a make-shift curtained stage.*)

JOHN: In West Virginia. Way back in the hills. When I noticed stuck on a tree—. Look at that!

(*JOHN points, they all look.*)

ALICE: A theater bill? Way out here?

BUCK: They got theater even here it seems.

THOMAS: *("Reads")* "Opera Mad or Romeo and Juliet with Laura Agnes."

JOHN: It starts at seven.

EDWARD: Could be worth a laugh.

KATE: *(Quietly:)* Laura Agnes??

(They all turn to KATE.)

KATE: I knew a Laura Agnes. She was perhaps the greatest, most—delicate actresses I've ever seen. I thought she was dead. Or—maybe a star in England? At the height of her fame—she suddenly abandoned the stage—and in the middle of a performance.

THOMAS: She just walked—?

KATE: Yes. While doing Juliet.

ALICE: She's doing Juliet—.

KATE: There was talk that her Romeo had been found with another...

(KATE looks at HANK, then away. Others try not to notice.)

KATE: So—this is where she's been all these years. I'd give anything to see her play.

(The curtain slowly starts to part.)

BUCK: It's starting...

(They take their seats. LAURA AGNES appears on stage.)

KATE: That's her.

SUSAN: She's so beautiful.

THOMAS: Sh-sh...

LAURA: *(In a high operatic voice:)* La la la.
(She suddenly turns.)
Romeo? Is that you, Romeo?
(A life-sized dummy of a man is thrown on stage. She looks

at it, then tenderly picks him up: she will speak both parts.)
By whose direction found'st thou out this place.
(Moving Romeo's head as she speaks:)
(As Romeo) By love, that first did prompt me to inquire.
(As Juliet)
Thou knowest the mask of night is on my face.
(She makes an evil/crazed face.)

(The acting troupe look at each other and move uncomfortably in their seats.)

LAURA: *(As Juliet)*
Else would a maiden blush bepaint my cheek
For that which thou hast heard me
(Screams into the dummy's ear:)
Speak to-night!!
Fain would I dwell on form—.
(She violently throws down the dummy.) Fein, fein Deny.
(She kicks the dummy.)
What I have spoke; but farewell compliment!
*(She kicks the dummy off. But it comes flying back.
She looks at it, touched by its return:)*
Do you love me??
(She picks up the dummy and kisses it, tongues it.)
I know thou wilt say—
(She plays with the dummy's crotch.)
At lover's perjuries,
They say jove laughs.
(She fondles its crotch.)
Or if thou thinkest I am too quickly won.
I'll frown.
(She begins kissing its chest.)
And be—perverse.
(She buries her face in the dummy's crotch.)

(The lights slowly fade on LAURA.)

(The troupe is stunned; pause.)

(Then as if nothing had just happened, they sing and begin to walk again:)

ALL: *(Singing)*
Woke up one morning
On the Chisolm Trail
With a rope in my hand
And a cow by the tail
Come a-ty-yi-yippi
Yippi-a yippi-a
Come a-ty-yi-yippi
Yippi-a!

(As they walk, they speak to us:)

JOHN: We crossed the Plains States of Ohio, Indiana and Illinois.

BUCK: Farm states.

THOMAS: Free states.

ALICE: The rustling we heard one night in the bushes, was but escaping Negroes, heading north.

SUSAN: And not the wolves or rabid dogs we feared.

GEORGE: We crossed wide open fields where broken and twisted stalks left from last autumn's corn, were now buried, entombed in ice.

THOMAS: We crossed open spaces.

EDWARD: And towns were we paid two cents each for a bath. Three cents with soap.

KATE: A fox followed us for days. Then was gone.

SUSAN: We watched flocks of birds, so thick they changed the color of the sky.

JOHN: Found earth so black and rich it seemed half animal.

ALICE: Then at last we reached the mighty Missouri.

THOMAS: And our gateway to the West!

(They stop walking. They are confused:)

(In front of them [unseen] the noise of crowds, music, partying, singing, etc.)

JOHN: What's all that?

BUCK: We're not alone.

THOMAS: Who are they?

GEORGE: *(To us)* There upon the river's bank was—a city of tents.

EDWARD: *(To us)* Filled we soon were to learn—with actors from around he globe.

HANK: *(To us)* Acrobats from Spain.

KATE: *(To us)* Jugglers from the Court of the Tsar.

RUTH: *(To us)* The famed Ravel Mime Troupe of Paris, France.

THOMAS: I don't understand. Why are they here?

(RICE approaches them:)

RICE: For the same reason you are, Thomas Jefferson Calhoun Star Troupe.

(All turn to RICE.)

RICE: They've heard the stories about the hunger for shows in the West.

THOMAS: Then why are they all *camped* here? Why aren't they on their way—?

RICE: The thaw.

ALICE: What??

RICE: They're all waiting for the thaw. You can't cross the Great Plains and Deserts and Mountains without a thaw.

(RICE walks off, leaving them alone.)

(The music, etc, continues off. At first the troupe doesn't know what to do. then one by one they start to set their things down.)

BUCK: There doesn't seem to be a lot of room down there. I guess we have to camp up here...

(Others nod, they begin to settle down.)

(BUCK has started to strum his guitar.)

(It becomes the evening.)

JOHN: *(To no one in particular)* So how long before there's a—thaw??

(It is now their campsite:)

(KATE lies with her head on HANK's lap, looking up at the stars.)

(BUCK is trying to teach both SUSAN and JOHN a new song on the guitar.)

(GEORGE tries to rest.)

(Others are gone.)

(RICE returns and watches them for a moment, then to us:)

RICE: While waiting for the snow to melt, early spring, on the banks of the Missouri River. *(He watches for a moment more then leaves.)*

ALICE: *(Off, calls:)* Thomas?!

BUCK: *(Showing SUSAN a chord)* Like this.

(SUSAN tries the chord, giggles. JOHN tries to "help." he reaches around her, touches her—they are flirting.)

BUCK: *(To SUSAN:)* You're not paying attention.

(ALICE enters.)

ALICE: Has anyone seen my husband?

BUCK: He went with—.

(JOHN kicks him.)

JOHN: No. We haven't. Seen him.

HANK: Need something, Alice?

ALICE: That Ravel Mime Troupe was supposed to do a show tonight. Thomas said we'd go. *(She looks off, then heads to look in another direction.)*

BUCK: *(To* JOHN*:)* Why did you kick me?

GEORGE: *(Suddenly sits up)* Can't they shut that child up?

(Others look at each other. They hear nothing but the general noise from the other camps.)

SUSAN: *(Finally)* What child, George?

JOHN: *(Reaching around* SUSAN *to strum the guitar and flirt)* Let me try that again.

*(*JOHN *touches* SUSAN's *hair, she looks into his eyes, then both self-consciously realize that the others are watching them.)*

JOHN: *(Suddenly stands)* Anyone else feel like a walk? Buck?

(Before BUCK *can answer:)*

JOHN: Susan?

SUSAN: *(Jumping up too quickly)* I would like a walk. Thank you. *(To the others)* It's a pretty night. *(Louder to the others)* We're just going to take a walk.

*(*SUSAN *and* JOHN *go off, trying not to hurry.)*

KATE: Young love.

*(*HANK *leans down and kisses* KATE*.)*

GEORGE: *(Suddenly standing)* Oh God. Hear that?

KATE: Hear what??

GEORGE: *(Listening intently:)* That goddamn child screaming.

(HANK and KATE listen.)

KATE: I don't hear a child... George?? I don't hear—? George?

HANK: He doesn't hear you. When he's concentrating he hears nothing.

KATE: How do you know?

HANK: I've acted with him.

GEORGE: Can't they shut that child up?! Goddamn children and their little buttons. I have to go talk to those parents. *(He hurries off.)*

KATE: *(Straining to hear the child)* I still don't hear—.

HANK: I don't think I've ever seen so many stars in the sky.

KATE: You're not looking at the sky.

(HANK and KATE kiss. Feeling uncomfortable, BUCK stands and "yawns".)

BUCK: Well, goodnight.

(HANK and KATE are still kissing. BUCK yawns again.)

BUCK: Good—night. *(He goes.)*

KATE: I hope we didn't drive him off.

HANK: You liar.

(KATE flinches.)

HANK: What is it? I told you we should see a doctor.

KATE: *(Sitting up)* I'm fine. I'm over it. I don't need a doctor. I must have eaten something. *(She looks at him and smiles.)* We will be fine. I'm feeling better than I've ever felt in my life.

HANK: Me too.

KATE: And you don't even want a drink anymore, do you?

(HANK *shakes his head.*)

(ALICE *returns:*)

ALICE: Still no Thomas?

KATE: No, Alice. Sorry.

(ALICE *looks off, she is very anxious.*)

ALICE: It's not like him.

HANK: (*To* ALICE, *starting to get up*) Would like me to go and—?

ALICE: No. No.

(HANK *sits back down.*)

KATE: I'm sure he's fine. Why don't you sit with us, Alice. Look at all those stars.

(ALICE *hesitates, then:*)

ALICE: No. I should go to bed.

KATE: Maybe we all should get to bed—.

(THOMAS, *with* RUTH *on his arm, enters. They are laughing, giggling. With them is a tall man with a stove-pipe hat. They have just come from the mime troupe and are imitating them.*)

(*They stop when they see the others looking at them.*)

RUTH: (*Guilty*) We—just saw the French Mime Troupe show. (*She laughs.*)

ALICE: The Mime Troupe?? Thomas? You saw that show? Is that where you've been? With her?

RUTH: It was so stupid, Alice, you didn't miss a thing.

(RUTH *looks to* THOMAS *who doesn't say anything.*)

RUTH: (*To* THOMAS) Did she? Did she?

ALICE: Then it's a good thing I didn't bother to go. (*Upset, hurries off*)

(*Awkward moment*)

RUTH: *(Guiltily to the others)* She didn't miss anything.

(Suddenly the man, ABE, *recognizes* HANK:*)*

ABE: Mister Daley? Hank Daley. And— *(Mouths: "Kate Denim")* I don't believe it.

THOMAS: He wanted to meet you both. He's a theater lover, he says. Aren't you, Abe?

ABE: *(To* HANK*)* I saw your Macbeth.

THOMAS: Abe's a lawyer.

ABE: "Kill all the lawyers!" *(Laughs at his joke)* Shakespeare got that right! From Illinois... Just— *(Points in the direction of Illinois.)*

KATE: How do you do.

ABE: *(Star-struck)* I've seen—your Desdemona.

THOMAS: He's been hanging round for days. I promised to show him costumes...

ABE: I hope I'm not intruding—.

THOMAS: No, really, it's—.

ABE: I love theater.

HANK: *(To* KATE*)* So he said...

THOMAS: Our wagon's over here...

(They are heading off toward the wagon.)

ABE: May I touch the properties?

(They are gone. HANK *and* KATE *look at a guilty-looking* RUTH.*)*

RUTH: *(Finally)* He asked me to go to the show. I didn't do anything.

*(*GEORGE *returns now with a bloody nose.)*

KATE: What happened to you?

GEORGE: *(Stops, listens)* Listen. See, they can keep their goddamn child quiet. *(He lies back where he was.)*

(EDWARD *enters laughing with a male friend. He has his arm around him. When he sees the others, he removes his arm:*)

EDWARD: *(Explaining)* A fellow Englishman.

KATE: How do you do.

MAN: From Liverpool. *(To* EDWARD*)* I've never heard that accent before.

GEORGE: He's from "Summersets".

(MAN is confused.)

RUTH: *(Interested)* An actor?

EDWARD: He's with a whole company—.

MAN: Edward and I just met. I admired his eyelashes.

RUTH: *(Uninterested now)* I see.

KATE: *(To* HANK*)* So have I.

EDWARD: We were just taking a walk.

MAN: Lovely night. A lot of stars.

KATE: There are.

RUTH: Enjoy your walk.

(As they head off, ABE *and* THOMAS *return from the wagon with bits of costume, ruffs, a sword, skull. They enter talking.)*

ABE: *(To* THOMAS*)* So this other lawyer, whenever I quote Shakespeare—he has two quotes. I give three, he gives four. Five, six. Twelve, thirteen. I can't win. I'm standing there before the judge—who knows what he could be thinking—and I know he's got me, this lawyer. I shake his hand and offer to buy him a drink...

(ABE realizes the others are listening to him.)

THOMAS: Abe's telling me about how—.

ABE: It's not that interesting, I'm sure you've got better—.

THOMAS: No, tell us.

ABE: So I said to this lawyer-—how come living out here in nowhere—their courthouse wasn't more than a mud hut—you know all this Shakespeare? And he sort of smiles at me, pours himself another drink, and tells me this story. *(To the others)* You know who Johnny Appleseed was?

KATE: Sure. He went around the country—.

ABE: Around America.

HANK: Planting apple trees.

THOMAS: Seeds. Not trees.

ABE: Well—it's sort of like that—the man said to me. In fact, he was even a friend of Appleseed's, this man. His name was Arthur—Arthur Shakespeare.

KATE: Any relation to—?

ABE: A direct descendent. Direct.

GEORGE: In America?

ABE: Oh, a lot of 'em got to America, he told me. Once they closed those theatres down in England, they had to go somewhere, didn't they? So a number of Shakespeares snuck out of that country, got themselves on some boats, and headed for America. Arthur was just one of them—the best known, maybe, or so it turned out—but still just one.

(ALICE appears in the distance.)

THOMAS: *(Seeing his wife)* Alice, come and listen to this.

(As ABE continues, ALICE joins the group, though keeps a distance from her husband.)

ABE: And just as Appleseed had his burlap bag of seed, Arthur had his bag of plays. His great relative's plays—*Hamlet, Merchant of Venice, Katherine and Petruchio*. All of them were in there.

KATE: And what did he do with his bag of plays, Abe?

(HANK *stands.*)

HANK: I should get the others. They should hear this. *(As he heads off:)* Susan! Buck! Edward! John!

ABE: *(To* KATE*)* He—planted them. *(To the others:)* Everywhere he goes, first only in the East of course, where he started out. Every time he stopped for food or drink or rest, he left a play behind, and pretty soon—

*(The others—*SUSAN, JOHN, BUCK, EDWARD *and the* MAN *are entering with* HANK *to listen.* HANK *has been explaining to them what abe has been saying.)* —because he traveled a lot—the East was pretty rich with plays. As you know. That's true, isn't it?

KATE: *(Smiles and nods)* Yes. That's true.

ABE: But then Arthur set his sights on the whole rest of America—on the farms, and the valleys, the fields, the plains, the mountains and the deserts. And so he planted more and more, planted everywhere he went until now with children and grandchildren and even great grandchildren, he reached the Pacific Ocean— with its blue water, and big tumbling waves, he reached the beach...

*(*ALL *are sitting now, circled around abe, listening.)*

ABE: ...and there with his family beside him, his big ol' arms spreading from him like an eagle does, he turned and looked back at all he had accomplished. And even he was amazed—for as far as one could see, there were plays—growing taller and freer than they'd ever growed before. Forests, bending in the wind's breezes, like dancers, like actors. *(Short pause)* Planted along river banks—to stop erosion. In rows through deserts to stop the same thing there. Planted in clumps to give protection, to give shade—to give the eye the sight of beauty. Planted to be harvested, and burned for heat, for warmth and comfort in this desolate and unfriendly world. Harvested for homes, roofs, and pulped into books for knowledge and learning, for understanding. And for the pursuit of happiness. The pursuit of truth. The pursuit—of ourselves.

(Silence. Wind)

*(*ABE *takes off his hat, and now he is* RICE*:)*

RICE: *(To us)* With the thaw the Thomas Jefferson Calhoun Star Troupe joined the mass exodus across the Missouri River.

(The others stand and continue the journey, walking. they speak to us.)

RUTH: The river did not part—so the local ferrymen did a whirlwind business that day.

BUCK: And the next.

*(*GEORGE *digs a hole in the earth with a shovel, as the others continue:)*

HANK: Somewhere, a few hundred miles or so across the Kansas Territories—

KATE: Kate woke sick again.

SUSAN: Susan, her and Hank's confidant, could keep silent no more. *(To the others:)* She's expecting a child.

(Reactions from the others: joy, excitement, concern.)

ALICE: *(To us)* The first thought was to turn back.

KATE: For God's sake why? So far this trip's been easier than a late afternoon drive down Broadway.

JOHN: Everyone laughed at that.

HANK: An omen, we agreed: a coming birth to match the rebirth of our lives.

JOHN: We doted on Kate.

KATE: Being Kate, I resisted. I'm not sick.

SUSAN: She said.

ALICE: Her green eyes glowed, her cheeks ruddy; this was not illness, this was life.

RUTH: Then one night, while winding our way along with tens of other wagons—a train of wagons, we called it, Kate woke.

(KATE *screams in pain.*)

ALICE: Her lap—bloody. Their child—miscarried.

(*No one knows what to do, then:*)

THOMAS: Thomas ordered the wagons stopped—to give Kate rest, relief from the bumps and gullies of the hard road.

HANK: Hank held her all night in his arms, comforting her, and himself. (*He holds her.*)

THOMAS: We'll catch up.

GEORGE: (*Digging*) And they'll wait.

BUCK: Though none of us believed that for a second.

HANK: Hank kept the pace as slow as possible, pleaded for regular stoops, so Kate could lay out in the prairie grass, and the cool spring air.

KATE: Of course no one knew—or could have had the chance to see, not even Hank these days, until one morning, bathing me—.

SUSAN: I noticed—between her legs—blood. Discolored blood, and a swollenness causing a pain which Kate had tried to hide—even from herself.

THOMAS: Until the pain was too much—and every moment, every foot we crept across the plain was accompanied by—

(KATE screams. She screams again.)

(HANK tries to take KATE's hand.)

GEORGE: *(Digging)* A doctor, so he claimed to be, was found in a nearby crossroads. He'd been out in the fields—doctoring his sheep.

EDWARD: He was filthy.

RUTH: And I think—drunk.

HANK: He doctored my Kate.

(KATE groans in pain.)

ALICE: And she got worse. The blood poured and didn't stop.

SUSAN: Susan nursed her for two days without sleeping.

BUCK: When finally the agony settled, like a storm ending.

THOMAS: Thank god. We all said. *(Short pause)* She is at peace.

(The others stand as for a funeral. KATE gets up and leaves the stage—no one else notices this. GEORGE has finished shoveling.)

GEORGE: Between the year 1849 and 1853 one grave was dug, on average, for every eighty yards between the Missouri River and California.

JOHN: John Gough said the service—what he remembered of it from playing a minister in *The Witch Of Windermere*.

(Wind, as they stand before the "grave".)

SUSAN: Two weeks passed and no sign of anyone.

(They are walking again.)

ALICE: Not even recent tracks.

RUTH: Though there was the occasional prairie house.

EDWARD: Upon approaching the first of these log cabins, they heard the slam of hardwood shutters, a few muffled shouts, and the greeting of the barrel of a shotgun.

BUCK: They kept their distance.

THOMAS: One night, to keep up their spirits, they rehearsed. In costume.

(It is evening, on a hillside near their campsite. From the [unseen] camps, BUCK plays a lonely tune on the harmonica.)

(HANK and SUSAN, now dressed in bits of costume, rehearse. She holds a book; he knows his part.)

HANK: But here she comes, and now, Petruchio, speak.
Good morrow—Kate, for that's your name I hear.

SUSAN: *(Reading)*
Well have you heard, but something hard of hearing.
They all me Katherine that do talk of me.

HANK: You lie, in faith for you are called plain—Kate,
And bonny Kate, and sometimes Kate the...
(He can't continue, he tries not to choke up.)

SUSAN: Let's stop. It can't be a lot of fun acting with me anyway.

(HANK shakes his head—that is not the reason.)

(Pause)

(They listen to the music, then:)

SUSAN: I miss her too. I can't tell you how many times I saw her on the stage. She was so beautiful. Such grace. And wit. This *(The costume)* —was hers?

(HANK nods.)

SUSAN: It doesn't fit me. I'm not Kate Denim.

HANK: I don't think I properly thanked you for what you did—the nursing—all those weeks. I was in awe

of you. Thank you. *(He looks off.)* It's better to work.
(He taps her book.) The dress—can be made to fit. *(Starts again:)*
Myself am moved to woo thee for my wife

SUSAN:
Moved? In good time: let him that moved you hither
Remove you hence. I knew you at the first,
You were moveable.

HANK: Why? What's a moveable?

SUSAN: A joint-stool.

HANK: Thou hast hit it: come sit on me.

(HANK and SUSAN are beginning to smile, to enjoy each other.)

SUSAN: Asses are made to bear, and so are you.

HANK: Women are made to bear, and so are you.

SUSAN: No such jade as you, if me you mean."
I don't understand, what's "jade"?

HANK: You've just called me a broken down old horse.

SUSAN: I like that.

HANK: Alas, good Kate, I will not burden thee
For knowing thee to be but young and light.

(HANK sips from a flask, he's drinking again.)

SUSAN: *("Running away")*
Too light for such a swain as you to catch,
And yet as heavy as my weight should be.

HANK: Should be? Should—buzz!

SUSAN: Well ta'en, and like a buzzard.

HANK: O slow-winged turtle!
Shall a buzzard take thee?

SUSAN: Ay for a turtle, as he takes a buzzard

(SUSAN touches HANK and "runs away".)

(JOHN *appears at a distance, and watches.*)

HANK: Come, come, you wasp, i' faith you are too angry.

SUSAN: If I be waspish best beware my sting.

(HANK *comes to* SUSAN, *she does not run away.*)

HANK: My remedy is then to pluck it out.

SUSAN: Ay, if the fool could find it where it lies.

HANK:
Who knows not where a wasp does wear his sting?
In his tail.

SUSAN: In his tongue.

(HANK *and* SUSAN *are very close.*)

(ALICE *now enters from the campsite. She too watches from a distance, she also notices* JOHN *watching.*)

HANK: Whose tongue?

SUSAN: Yours, if you talk of tales, and so farewell.

HANK: What, with my tongue in your tail?

(SUSAN *kisses* HANK. *He kisses back.*)

JOHN: *(Interrupting)* Susan?!

(HANK *and* SUSAN *break apart and see* JOHN.)

ALICE: Rehearsing, are we?

(HANK *and* SUSAN *see* ALICE *for the first time.*)

(*Off,* BUCK *has started playing a rousing country tune.*)

SUSAN: *(To* HANK) Listen to what Buck's playing. Let's go back and listen.

(SUSAN *hurries off.* HANK *hesitates, looks at* JOHN *and* ALICE, *and self-consciously follows* SUSAN *off.*)

(*Pause*)

(ALICE approaches JOHN who is now staring off at the hills. It is getting dark.)

ALICE: Look at those hills. They call them the Black Hills, don't they? I think Thomas said that—I heard him telling Ruth. The Black Hills. *(She looks back at the camp.)* He's dancing with her now. My husband. I don't know what to do, John. Tell me something—*her husband* doesn't seem to even notice. Or is it care? Why is that?

(JOHN looks at ALICE.)

JOHN: I don't know.

ALICE: He doesn't act like a husband.

JOHN: No, he doesn't.

(Pause)

ALICE: The way those hills catch the moonlight. Like a backdrop. Like a stage. I suppose so far—all that we've seen—what amazes me the most is the way that it all looks like a stage. One can imagine a scenic painter on his ladder—.

JOHN: I think I saw some light over there. *(He points.)* And smoke. That's what brought me up here.

ALICE: I see.

JOHN: So—we can't be far behind the other wagons. We'll catch up.

(Pause. There is an odd silence. BUCK has stopped playing. It takes them a moment to notice.)

ALICE: Maybe I won't even sleep in the wagon tonight. Let him have it alone. Let him do what he wants.

JOHN: Buck has stopped.... *(Looks off toward the camp)* The fire's out.

(It gets darker.)

ALICE: What happened to the moon?

JOHN: Clouds passing.

ALICE: I can hardly see. We better go back whether we want to or not.

JOHN: Yes. Let's go...

(Suddenly, in the dark, figures grab ALICE and JOHN, cover their mouths, and as they struggle and try and scream they are carried away.)

(Drums)

(The entire troupe find themselves inside a large tepee. As they huddle together:)

THOMAS: The lights and wisps of smoke seen from their hilltop hadn't been from the wagon train after all, but from a two-thousand-strong Cheyenne Indian village.

GEORGE: They were taken to a large tepee, on the extreme edge of this town.

BUCK: And left, isolated there, alone, except for the shadows of their guards outside.

(Drums continue off; they are scared.)

HANK: The sun rose.

SUSAN: We could feel this through the animal skins.

ALICE: There were furs for rugs.

EDWARD: Wool blankets of reds, purples, greens—like a sunset.

BUCK: We huddled, rarely speaking.

(Short pause.)

THOMAS: After hours of this terror, Thomas, being the elder, and having been sent to meet the Chief returned. *(He stands before the others:)* I said—my name is Thomas Calhoun. I come from New York.

HANK: Do they speak English?

THOMAS: There's a white man with him. A buffalo hunter. Bill. He translated.

(Lights up on BILL. BILL *translates for the chief, who remains [unseen] outside the tepee.)*

THOMAS: We—mean no harm, I said. We don't wish to hurt anyone. And hope, no one wishes to hurt us.

BILL: *("Translating")* I hope that is true. I hope we shall not have to kill you too.

JOHN: These are killer Indians!

ALICE: Be quiet.

BILL: *("Translating")* A year ago two families of settlers arrived in our hills. They arrived with the moon, they came with horses, a wagon each. One mother held a small child, and it cried. We heard this in the night. A crying baby, crying like our babies cry. Most of my people had never seen white men before. Only Bill. Who came to learn our ways. We have much to teach the white man, we know—and now they have come to us to learn, we decided. We watch their houses built. We offer food. Their smiles are like our smiles. Inside one house this baby still cries. Then a young woman from our village—

THOMAS: The Chief's favorite—I learn.

BILL: *("Translating")* She goes to help this baby. She has ways with children. They baby is hot. Red, in patches on its body. Finally, the baby is well and happy, thanks to my daughter. *(Short pause)* The child had what you told me Bill is called—measles. Soon my daughter is dead. Her sister. One brother. And wife. We bury...

THOMAS: One thousand.

BILL: *("Translating")* We bury and bury.

THOMAS: That's when I looked around me and realized there wasn't another Indian within fifty yards of me.

SUSAN: They're scared that we have measles?

BILL: *("Translating")* The settlers" houses, we burned. The settlers fought this and died. Only then did the—measles—go away.

BUCK: But we don't have measles, you told him that?

BILL: *("Translating")* We have followed you for some time. One of our young men watched as you buried a body. Without—burning it.

HANK: Oh god.

THOMAS: They dug up Kate, and burned her body.

BILL: *("Translating")* You bring death—you will die if you do.

THOMAS: And then—he left.

(Lights out on the CHIEF *and* BILL.)

(No one knows what to say.)

*(*BILL *suddenly enters, carrying blankets. He startles them, they shriek.)*

THOMAS: It's Bill! It's Bill.

BILL: If one of you so much as sneezes, I'll kill you myself. Take off your clothes.

RUTH: What??

BILL: All of them. And put these blankets over you.

SUSAN: I don't understand.

HANK: I think we're in some sort of quarantine.

BILL: Everything gets burned. Chief's orders. I'll try and get you some Indian clothes later.

ALICE: Burned?

BUCK: We have other clothes in our wagon.

ALICE: We have our costumes.

BILL: Your wagon got pushed over the side of a cliff. What do you mean "costumes"?

BUCK: For our shows.

THOMAS: We're actors.

BILL: Actors??

GEORGE: On our way West. We're just passing through.

BILL: Why didn't you tell me you were actors?!

THOMAS: What difference would that have made?

BILL: I've been telling the injuns for years: your food's great, love the buffalo; your women are attractive; you got great story tellers, funnier than hell. I love the music. *(He points out the drumming.)* They got sports better than we got. Everything's here, I tell `em— except for one thing. *(Short pause for effect:)* Theater. They don't have theater! Preferably, I tell `em— Shakespeare. You folks wouldn't know *King Lear* by any chance?

BUCK: *Lear*?

THOMAS: We can do *Lear*.

BILL: I saw it as a kid and it just stuck with me. I think I must have read it now a million times, I pretty much know it by heart.

SUSAN: Buck, it's just like your story.

BUCK: *(Stunned)* I know. I know.

HANK: You really think the Chief would—enjoy —*King Lear*?

BILL: Of course injuns don't have the first idea about owning property, let alone dividing it up. Still—they got daughters, so I think he'll have a good time.

(BILL goes off. The others are stunned.)

(They look at the blankets and skins BILL *brought—these will be their costumes. They look at each other, then:)*

HANK: So—it was *King Lear*. In what, in all probability, was the first ever performance of this play among the Black Hills of the Dakotas, inside a tepee.

(The drumming continues off. They set up a curtain across the tepee—what we see will be "backstage".)

(They are nervous as they get ready.)

(In silence they hand out the various skins and blankets— deciding who gets one for which role.)

*(*BUCK *off to one side, lost in his thoughts, sings to himself:)*

BUCK: I started up the trail
October twenty-third...
(He hums the rest.)

SUSAN: *(What she can't stop thinking about, to* ALICE:*)*
They dug up Kate and burned her body...

ALICE: Stop thinking about it. Just stop thinking.

BUCK: *(As he fingers a "pretend" guitar)*
Come a-ty-yi-yippi
Yippi...[hums]

ALICE: *(Having watched* BUCK:*)* His guitar was in the wagon...

ALL: *(Sing nervously to themselves:)*
Come a-ty-yi-yippi
Yippi-a...

(They suddenly stop. The drumming has gotten much louder.)

GEORGE: The Chief doesn't even understand English.

EDWARD: *(Holding up some bit of fur)* Does this look more like Kent or Goneril?

*(*JOHN *is peeking around the curtain.)*

(The drumming suddenly stops.)

JOHN: He's here. He's here.

(A few peek around the curtain.)

(We hear the CHIEF clap his hands three times. The actors look at each other, then THOMAS nods to BUCK who begins to play the harmonica and the play begins.)

(THOMAS, as Lear, and the three daughters [RUTH, ALICE and SUSAN] go through the curtain and onto the "stage".)

EDWARD: *(To GEORGE)* I am so damn scared....

ALICE: *(Peeks back through the curtain:)* He's smiling. The Chief's smiling.

(From "the stage" we hear THOMAS as Lear: "Nothing will come of nothing.")

RUTH: *(Coming back through the curtain, to us:)* When the King banished his daughter, the Chief tried to stop the play.

(SUSAN/Cordelia comes through the curtain.)

EDWARD: *(Peeking through)* Why's he doing that?

ALICE: He looks upset. *(To SUSAN)* He's trying to get you back. He knows Lear's made a mistake.

EDWARD: *(Peeking)* Bill's coaxed him back into his seat.

(They all breathe a little easier.)

SUSAN: *(To us)* And as the play continued, the Chief's interest only grew.

(JOHN as the fool is doing a little "dance" on stage.

EDWARD: He's laughing. Why's he laughing so hard at that?

HANK: He's a king himself. So maybe he recognized something.

THOMAS: *(To us)* On the cliffs of Dover as blind Gloucester—

(GEORGE *"enters" the stage as blind Gloucester.*)

THOMAS: —falls a few feet—though a mile in his mind—Bill tried to translate.

SUSAN: *(Peeking through the curtain)* He's brushing Bill away. He understands.

HANK: And when at last a father carries his daughter in his arms, his favorite daughter—who is dead...

(THOMAS *lifts up* SUSAN, *wobbles a bit.*)

SUSAN: Don't drop me.

JOHN: Go!!

(JOHN *opens the curtain for* THOMAS/*Lear carrying* SUSAN/*Cordelia.*)

THOMAS: *(Entering)* "Howl, howl, howl, howl! O you are men of stones..."

HANK: The Chief bowed his head, covered his face in his hands, and wept. Until the end.

(Silence)

(BUCK *has stopped playing. They pull open the curtain, and we see the* CHIEF *in tears.*)

BUCK: We could see in the eyes the effect the play had had upon him.

SUSAN: A trembling hand. A dry throat.

ALICE: He stopped Bill's translation halfway through the play, and just watched, understanding, it seems, everything—across worlds, time, languages, until being touched to his soul.

GEORGE: He came to each one of us.

(CHIEF *gets up and goes to the actors.*)

EDWARD: No longer afraid—to touch. No longer scared of us.

HANK: And one after one—

SUSAN: He hugged me.

(CHIEF hugs SUSAN.)

GEORGE: And me.

(CHIEF hugs GEORGE.)

THOMAS: And me.

(CHIEF huns THOMAS.)

(Short pause)

THOMAS: And then—he was shot.

(Gunshot. And the CHIEF falls dead.)

(The others scream and run for safety, as BUCK speaks to us.)

BUCK: At first the white settlers thought we were Indians too, I suppose because of the clothes. I screamed for them to stop. They couldn't hear—or chose not to. I recall one white man in particular. I watched him with his long shiny sword approach a young Indian woman—her breasts bare of course—and stab into her chest, splitting her. He twisted that sword and plunged, until he could lift this lifeless body up off her feet, and bounce her, like a wooden toy. *(Short pause.)* It was in this man's house—days later—in which I awoke.

(Bedroom of a farmhouse: BUCK is in a bed, and "MOTHER" stands over him, rubbing a wet cloth on his head as he wakes up:)

BUCK: *(Startled and scared)* Who are you?!

MOTHER: I am your Mother, dear Ezekiel.

BUCK: What? Where are my friends? What's happened to our troupe?

MOTHER: All dead. Only my dear Ezekiel has survived. Thanks to God. And to my husband.

("FATHER" *appears.*)

MOTHER: Who recognized the white skin in that Indian filth. Now will you take them off? Each time I tried, you fought me.

(*He starts to take off his Indian costume and put on clean clothes.*)

BUCK: How long have I been here?

MOTHER: Six days, hasn't it been, husband?

FATHER: (*Touches* BUCK's *face*) Ezekiel.

BUCK: My name's not—.

FATHER: It is now.

MOTHER: We have long prayed, Ezekiel, for a son. And now we have one. Try and sleep.

(FATHER *and* MOTHER *go.*)

BUCK: (*To us*) I soon learned that my "mother" and "father" belonged to a kind of religious community which banned all physical contact between men and women.

(*As* MOTHER *returns:*)

BUCK: (*To* MOTHER) But then how do you have children?

(MOTHER *smiles.*)

BUCK: You don't. You have to wait until God—or your husband—finds some...

MOTHER: That's right.

BUCK: How many children are there in this community?

MOTHER: We are the youngest here. But now there is Ezekiel.

BUCK: But I'm an actor, I can't stay here.

MOTHER: There are no "actors" in our community. Nor theater. God forbids "theater", as both a waste of precious time—when one could be working—and as an expression of pride and the sin of vanity. You aren't vain, are you, Ezekiel?

BUCK: (Smiling) I can proudly say—I don't have a single vain bone in my body.

(MOTHER hits BUCK across the head.)

MOTHER: We shall cure you of this and all other sins. (She goes.)

BUCK: (To us) And she wasn't kidding. Mother and Father slept for something like three hours a day—in the same bed by the way, I peeked, but with a thick board down the middle. And the rest of the time—

(MOTHER returns and hands BUCK a hoe.)

BUCK: We worked.

(BUCK hoes. FATHER approaches him with a rifle.)

BUCK: On breaks—ten minutes every four hours—I was given lessons.

(FATHER hands BUCK the gun.)

BUCK: I was taught how to shoot. (He shoots, and keeps shooting like a madman.) I was encouraged to draw pictures—of Indians and later niggers, and Father and I would go out and practice on these targets. (A couple of more shots. He hands the gun back to FATHER.) I was taught the truth.

FATHER: Who is your father?

BUCK: Earthly or heavenly?

FATHER: Heavenly.

BUCK: God is my father.

FATHER: And earthly?

BUCK: He's back in Ohio—.

(FATHER *hits* BUCK *across the head.*)

BUCK: You are my father. *(To us:)* I was taught love.

FATHER: Why did we have to kill those Indians?

BUCK: It was for their own good, Father. They had harmed white people, and must be sent to heaven.

(FATHER *hits* BUCK *again.*)

BUCK: *(Correcting himself)* Sent—away.

(FATHER *leaves.*)

BUCK: And so it would have been for the rest of my life, had not, one fine day before bed, Mother come to me with—

(MOTHER *enters with a large book.*)

MOTHER: The Family Bible. I'm putting you into it, Ezekiel. Now—what's the date of your baptism?

(BUCK *hesitates, then whispers in* MOTHER's *ear. She screams and hits him on the head.*)

BUCK: Perhaps the decent thing would have been just to lie and say I was baptized, but the truth, once you get to learning it, is hard to forget. *(He rubs his head.)* Fortunately for all of us, Father said—.

FATHER: *(Entering)* There's a revivalist coming to town this weekend, we'll get him to do the honors of God. And while we're at it, Mother—

BUCK: He continued.

FATHER: Why don't we give ourselves over one more time.

BUCK: For something like the forty-third time, I was to learn. *(Shrugs)* Saves taking a bath, I suppose. Anyway, off we went that Saturday morning to the local crawfish pond, which, I knew had plenty of snapping turtles—so I was actually looking forward to the show. And there we were standing in line, waiting for the minister when I saw something strange on Father's face.

(FATHER *stares off, angry.*)

FATHER: Mother, look over there. *(He is looking off.)* They have their nerve.

BUCK: And soon I saw what the problem was. Parishioners from an offshoot—the liberal wing of our church society—they still didn't touch, but they could sing—at funerals and baptisms, but not at weddings—had arrived too for communal baptism by the God-fearing revivalist preacher. And Father didn't like it.

FATHER: What are they here for?

MOTHER: The same as we are, I suppose, husband.

FATHER: They better not sing.

BUCK: *(To us)* I was too busy watching the tensions mount between these groups to notice the preacher's arrival.

(PREACHER *arrives wearing a big hat.*)

BUCK: Or pay attention to his blessings as I stood in line waiting to be dunked.

PREACHER: *(Head bowed)* We ask our Lord to forgive us our sins, as we, your tortured souls, howl, howl, howl. O we are men of stones!

(This gets BUCK's attention.)

BUCK: *(In a whisper, to us)* It's— *(To JOHN)* John!!

JOHN: Sh-sh.

BUCK: But before I could ask him anything, or think up a plan of escape—.

(Off, the "liberal" parishioners begin to sing Nearer My God To Thee.*)*

BUCK: The good Liberal people from the Other Valley began to sing. And Father grew incensed!

FATHER: *(Under his breath)* Stop that. Stop that...

MOTHER: Husband...

FATHER: *(Shouts)* Stop that, you hear me! You anti-Christs!

(FATHER pulls out a gun and shoots in the air. Others shoot back. He and MOTHER run off to fight.)

(Off—a gun battle. BUCK and JOHN watch in horror—hearing the screams and cries and the killing.)

(Stunned) Amidst the confusion, John Gough and I snuck away.

(Sounds of birds and wild animals as they go through "the woods".)

BUCK: We followed the stream feeding out of the pond for a mile or so—telling each other of our adventures and near escapes, pausing only once—when proceeded by a gush of red, Mother floated down the stream, her face up, her eyes red—much like:

JOHN: Ophelia.

BUCK: *(To JOHN)* Just like her.

(BUCK and JOHN "watch" the body go by:)

BUCK: If Ophelia were old and fat. Enjoy heaven, Mom!

(BUCK and JOHN continue to walk:)

BUCK: And then continued with our stories without missing so much as a another beat.

JOHN: *(To us)* And so we filled the next three days, until:

(RICE now dressed as a farmer, enters, dragging a beaten MAN along by a rope.)

RICE: They watched from a distance a man with a gun drag along by a rope, a beaten a filthy man.

(BUCK and JOHN "hide".)

JOHN: Who looked to all the world like—

BUCK: Poor Tom. His clothes torn, his face bloodied, and around his neck a sign which says:

RICE: *(Reads the sign around the MAN's neck)* "Pervert."

(RICE As the farmer kicks the MAN and throws him to the ground.)

RICE: Now get out of this territory. I so much as lay eyes on you again, and next time, I will cut your balls off.

(Another kick. The other MAN whimpers.)

JOHN: *(Still dressed as a PREACHER, comes out of hiding:)* What—has this poor man done?

RICE: It's not what he's done, Preacher, it's what he is.

(RICE Spits on the MAN, and goes.)

(BUCK comes out of hiding and sees:)

BUCK: It's—Edward!

(BUCK and JOHN hurry to EDWARD. Scared, he tries to fight them off.)

JOHN: It's all right. It's just us. John and Buck.

EDWARD: But—you're dead.

JOHN: Do we look dead?

(BUCK and JOHN untie EDWARD's hands; BUCK looks at the sign.)

BUCK: What happened? What's this about?

(JOHN Takes the sign off of EDWARD, and rips it up.)

JOHN: *(To EDWARD)* You don't have to say anything. Let's get you cleaned up. And out of here.

(EDWARD, his hands free, finds the mutilated copy of his Shakespeare in his pocket.)

EDWARD: My Shakespeare. Look what they did to my Shakespeare...

(BUCK and JOHN help EDWARD up.)

BUCK: People here don't deserve these plays.

EDWARD: *(He didn't hear)* What??

JOHN: Buck said—they don't deserve those plays.

EDWARD: That's not for us to say.

(Upstage the rest of the troupe appear, walking slowly, lost.)

BUCK: *(To us)* One by one we found each other.

(The others suddenly see BUCK, EDWARD and JOHN. For a moment they just stand and stare. They can't believe their eyes.)

BUCK: "Mother" had been wrong—they hadn't died. Like us, they had done what they had to, to survive!

(The others run to BUCK, EDWARD and JOHN—hug and touch each other; hold each other close.)

(Pause. As they look each other over.)

SUSAN: *(Finally)* We hid in the stream.

HANK: Under water. Breathing through reeds.

RUTH: Thomas held me. He kept screaming to the settlers:

THOMAS: 'We're white! We're white!'

HANK: You should have screamed, "We're actors!'

(The others laugh.)

EDWARD: Oh that would have done a lot of good.

ALICE: *(To us)* I followed Thomas and Ruth. I never let them out of my sight.

RUTH: *(To* EDWARD, *holding his face)* What happened to you?

JOHN: Don't ask.

BUCK: *(To* GEORGE*)* And you, George?

*(*GEORGE *doesn't respond.)*

BUCK: George??

SUSAN: He hasn't spoken since that horse kicked him in the head.

ALICE: *(To* EDWARD*)* Your wife missed you, Edward. I could tell.

EDWARD: My wife?? What wife??

ALICE: Ruth.

EDWARD: Ruth's not my wife. I thought everyone knew that. Didn't everyone know that?

(All nod, except for ALICE.*)*

ALICE: Oh God.

*(*ALICE *tries to grab her husband's arm, he won't let her. he stays with* RUTH.*)*

(They are all walking now.)

BUCK: I was taught the truth. I was taught love. I was taught to shoot.

JOHN: "I baptize thee in the name of—" And I forgot the line.

(Laughter)

JOHN: I made money. Nothing pays like religion.

THOMAS: Will you stop grabbing me, Alice? I'm helping Ruth walk.

(Pause. They walk in silence. Wind)

SUSAN: *(To* HANK*)* Last night you cried out in your sleep again.

HANK: Did I?

SUSAN: Cried out— "Kate". Why can't you just admit that you'll never love anyone else?

(HANK *looks at* SUSAN.)

SUSAN: Say it! Just say it!

(HANK *turns away.*)

(*Pause. They walk in silence. Wind*)

ALICE: It's cold.

EDWARD: What month is it anyway?

JOHN: Summer's over.

HANK: Just look at those trees.

THOMAS: Then the snow is coming.

(*Pause. They walk. Wind*)

SUSAN: Buck?

BUCK: What?

SUSAN: Tell us again what it'll be like.

BUCK: What what will be like?

SUSAN: Out West. In our theater.

BUCK: (*To us*) So they rested that night and circled around the fire, blankets over their shoulders to keep warm...

(*They sit around the "fire".*)

BUCK: ...snuggled together, and listened to what awaited them in California. (*To the others*) Candles stuck into empty bottles.

SUSAN: Different colors?

BUCK: Sure, why not?

JOHN: (*To the others, explaining*) They are the—.

THOMAS: Footlights.

BUCK: Who's telling this story?

(Laughter)

(GEORGE has been lying down.)

GEORGE: *(Gets up and speaks to us)* It wouldn't be until morning and the first rays of the dawn...

ALICE: *(To the others)* Sh-sh. Don't wake George. He needs his sleep.

GEORGE: ...that anyone would realize that George Demerest had passed away.

(GEORGE faces us and is suddenly lit by footlights.)

GEORGE: *(To us, as Lear)*
"Never, never, never, never, never.
Pray you, undo this—button."

(Sudden wild applause. GEORGE smiles, and leaves the stage.)

(BUCK now sits off to one side, mourning the death of GEORGE, playing on his harmonica. The others, still around the "fire" look at him. HANK gets up and goes and pats BUCK on the shoulder, and he begins to sing, and soon the others join in:)

HANK: Now come along boys
And listen to my tale

OTHERS: And I'll tell you about my troubles
On the Chisolm Trail
(They are walking again now.)
Come a-ty-yi-yippi
Yippi-a yippi-a
Come a-ty-yi yippi-yippi-a...

(They stop and look off and for a moment are speechless. then:)

BUCK: Oh my god...

THOMAS: *(To us)* The day we looked down upon the Great California Valley was the happiest I'd ever known.

JOHN: Eden. Or was it the Promised Land? Or Heaven.

ALICE: *(To us)* That day the sun broke through the clouds like you see in paintings. Rods of white light being thrown at the earth.

EDWARD: Smells. Of earth.

SUSAN: First we hard the birdsong. Hadn't heard a bird in such a long time.

BUCK: Then from somewhere deep down in the valley as if from in its soul...

(Distant banjo playing Arkansas Traveler, *like in* BUCK's *story.)*

RUTH: I needn't mention all we've gone through getting here.

THOMAS: Across the mountains.

EDWARD: All we saw along the way. Like those English actors, the same we'd met in Missouri? Found them frozen to death, dressed in layers of costume—Hamlet, Lear, the armor of Richard III.

THOMAS: Been slowed down by their wagons, got caught in a storm.

ALICE: And what storms they were, like white sheets thrown over your head. You saw nothing.

RUTH: We can't tell everything.

BUCK: How we slid halfway down one mountain. Buck had the idea of strapping boards onto his feet—interesting.

HANK: How we lived on melted snow for four days. Until we found a dead frozen horse.

BUCK: We ate no people. We promise.

JOHN: We talked about it though. Twice.

SUSAN: Or how we were attacked by wolves and a mountain lion. That's a very long story.

JOHN: How John Gough lost a finger.

THOMAS: Thomas part of an ear.

RUTH: And Ruth—three toes.

(Music gets louder.)

ALICE: How against reason and misfortune and eventually without hope, we climbed this last hill and saw this valley.

JOHN: And its towns.

(They point them out:)

RUTH: Mud Springs.

EDWARD: Rough and Ready.

ALICE: Rattlesnake.

THOMAS: Fiddletown.

HANK: Yankee Jim's

ALICE: And Red Dog. Red Dog.

BUCK: And music coming from each, as if beckoning— welcome. Glad to see you.

SUSAN: I can't describe the feeling.

RUTH: The women all thought of crying.

JOHN: And so did all the men.

THOMAS: But instead—all the way down that hill—we danced!!

(They dance "down the hill".)

THOMAS: And into—Red Dog, California!

(They stop, look out toward the audience at the town and its people.)

THOMAS: Population—

(Gunshot, sound of someone falling down dead.)

THOMAS: —fluid.

(Noise of a busy western town, wagons, shouts, music from a saloon, etc)

(As the troupe looks out:)

ALICE: Funny, at first glance, you'd never guess they were starved for Shakespeare.

THOMAS: *(Calls to an unseen man)* Excuse me—sir? We're—actors.

(The "man" obviously ignores him.)

HANK: *(Calls)* New York actors!

BUCK: Not the sort you've been used to doing your Shakespeare around here!

EDWARD: We actually know the words!

(EDWARD laughs at his joke. Clearly they are still being ignored.)

THOMAS: And the Oldfields here are from England! Say something in real English.

EDWARD: *(To the unseen man)* I think your California sunshine is so bloody refreshing after dreary old London town.

THOMAS: We're looking for a place to—establish ourselves. At least temporarily?

SUSAN: Until we see just how large a theatre we'll need.

RUTH: We need to get the word of mouth going.

THOMAS: You couldn't recommend...?

(He is getting nothing from the man. BUCK approaches another unseen person.)

BUCK: You! You! *(To the others:)* I've been waiting to ask this. To just pick a person at random and ask. *(To the person:)* We've been debating this among ourselves for the whole journey. *King Lear* or *Richard III*? Which, given your experience here, would you think would be the better to begin with? And I'm not just talking the most popular, am I?

ALICE: No. No.

BUCK: I mean—we mean to begin by giving the people here what they're most missing. Thereby, we hope, showing how willing we are to go that extra...

(The person has walked away.)

EDWARD: ...mile.

BUCK: *(Shouts at his back:)* King Lear. Richard. *(He weighs them with his hands.)*

SUSAN: *(Calls:)* You're the first we've asked!

(Pause. They awkwardly look around.)

BUCK: *(To us)* Eventually Thomas found a saloon keeper interested in putting on plays.

(They are all looking over the backroom of the saloon.)

JOHN: It's not bad. A little small.

ALICE: There's no stage.

THOMAS: We'll set one up.

SUSAN: Or seats.

BUCK: We can put in benches.

RUTH: It smells.

THOMAS: We'll open windows.

SUSAN: What windows?

EDWARD: Well, I like it. It has a certain... *(Can't find the word.)*

RUTH: Smell?

THOMAS: We split fifty-fifty with the owner. It's ours as soon as it's fixed up. He'll sell us what we need to fix it up for a hundred dollars.

ALICE: A hundred dollars? We don't have two dollars.

JOHN: Then what are we going to do?

SUSAN: Try another saloon.

BUCK: We've tried all the saloons in town. This was our last hope.

RUTH: *(To us)* Later that night, as the others slept, Ruth quietly snuck away. In the morning, she returned with—

(RUTH *holds out cash to the others.*)

THOMAS: A hundred dollars?? Where did you get a hundred dollars?

RUTH: I found it. I couldn't sleep, so I went for a walk and there in the street, I found... that.

THOMAS: You're the luckiest woman in the world. Isn't she, Alice?

RUTH: *(Holding* THOMAS*)* I think I am.

(RUTH *and* THOMAS *kiss.* ALICE *watches, others try not to notice.*)

BUCK: *(To us)* The theater was complete within a week.

RUTH: *(To everyone)* Look! I found more money—for the costumes!

JOHN: *(To us)* We flooded the town with bills announcing:

SUSAN: The Thomas Jefferson Calhoun Star Troupe!

THOMAS: Every time I walked past one, I stopped to read it.

ALICE: Direct from New York.

EDWARD: And London, England.

SUSAN: Presenting their internationally acclaimed production of William Shakespeare's—

HANK: *Richard the Third*!

(A curtain has been put up, and we are backstage. From the "audience" two or three people are applauding. We are at the end of the performance:)

SUSAN: No one—corrected us. As they had in Buck's story.

(The very light applause finishes, they notice.)

JOHN: No one—recited with us. No one.

ALICE: No gold was thrown. No rhythmic clapping.

HANK: *(As Richard III, coming out from "on stage")* The bottles with the candles have fallen over.

(No one knows what to say, then:)

BUCK: I think it went pretty well. What do you all think?

RUTH: Three stayed.

JOHN: One was passed out.

BUCK: No, he wasn't. That's just the way his eyes look. He had hooded eyes. *I* think he liked it.

EDWARD: Who were those people who came in and made that noise?

THOMAS: Did I imagine this or did they walk in, go into the corner, stand there for a while, and leave? *(Looks to the others)* Were they peeing?

SUSAN: I saw it.

ALICE: I heard it. In a pause.

JOHN: I think this is—was, before us—a sort of toilet.

ALICE: Explains the smell.

THOMAS: Why don't we all go get a drink and forget about tonight. Tomorrow's bound to be a better day.

BUCK: *(To us)* Thomas said, still acting.

EDWARD: Who has money for drink?

RUTH: I do! I found this! *(She takes out some bills.)* So I'll pay.

(RUTH and THOMAS head off. Before the others can follow:)

ALICE: *(Suddenly it bursts out)* How come she keeps finding money and I don't?! I go out into the street. I look. I don't find anything! It's not fair!

BUCK: Who's finding money, Alice?

ALICE: Ruth is. She is so lucky!

JOHN: *(After a look at the others)* Alice—Ruth is a whore. Didn't you know that?

ALICE: *(Stunned)* A...? But she came all the way from England.

EDWARD: Albany. We came from Albany.

(Then, when it all dawns on ALICE:)

ALICE: Does my husband know?

(The others look at each other, then:)

JOHN: You know—I don't think so.

(THOMAS and RUTH burst back in; THOMAS is clutching a theater bill.)

THOMAS: Look what's being handed out!

BUCK: It's a theater bill.

EDWARD: *(Reads)* "Edwin Booth!"

BUCK: *(Reads)* "Performing in—"

HANK: *(He doesn't have to read it)* Richard III.

ALICE: *(Reads, then:)* Where's Rough and Ready?

HANK: About a mile down the road.

BUCK: Booth? It must be someone pretending to be him.

HANK: No. It is him.

BUCK: I don't understand, how did Edwin Booth get out here?!

HANK: By boat.

(They all look at HANK.)

HANK: And across the Panama Isthmus. It now takes about thirty days—in comfort. They're all coming. The Starks. The Chapman Family. Even the young Batemans.

SUSAN: Good thing George—isn't here.

RUTH: *(To HANK)* How do you know all about this?

HANK: I ran into friends from New York this afternoon. I didn't want to say anything. I didn't want to spoil tonight.

JOHN: It'll be just like New York.

HANK: He's right.

EDWARD: Then who'll come and see us?

(Short pause)

HANK: Let's change, and take Ruth up on that drink. *(He moves away from the group and speaks to us:)* Susan soon found Hank's letter in the pocket of her costume. He had slipped it in there, at the end of the show.

(SUSAN takes out the letter and reads:)

SUSAN: "Dear Susan. I'm so sorry, but you are no Kate Denim." *(She breaks down crying.)*

HANK: *(To us)* Not exactly what I wrote, but I suppose it's what I meant.

JOHN: *(Holding SUSAN)* That son of a bitch.

HANK: *(As he takes off his costume, to us)* Hank that very afternoon had signed on with another troupe of actors, who having determined that California was now too crowded for them, were headed for Australia and the new gold rush there. Hank spent his last evening drunk and forgetting; by morning, his new friends would have to carry him to the ship that was taking them all away. *(He leaves the stage.)*

(SUSAN continues to cry.)

JOHN: *(To say something)* Wonder how Booth did tonight.

EDWARD: Probably like us. Thursday night. Who goes to the theater on a Thursday night?

RUTH: He sold out three days ago.

BUCK: See, I told you they loved Shakespeare out here.

(SUSAN cries. No one knows what to do.)

(RICE has entered and watched them, then:)

RICE: *(To us)* Just when you've hit rock bottom, a line appears and up you climb! *(He claps his hands.)* Excuse me! Pardon me! Listen. Listen! Who's in charge here?

THOMAS: *(Hesitates, then:)* I suppose I am, but...

RICE: Allow me to introduce myself. I am George Edgar Rice. And I just saw your show tonight.

RUTH: Which one were you?

RICE: I was one of those who came in to pee. Did you know this was the toilet?

BUCK: We guessed that.

RICE: But—I stayed. And for all I saw I have decided to spend my hard earned money by engaging your company in a production entirely financed by me.

(Stunned silence. They don't know what to say or think.)

SUSAN: What—sort of—play?

RICE: The one I have in mind is called—*Hamlet.*

EDWARD: *(He can hardly get the word out) Hamlet*???

THOMAS: Uh, Mister—

RICE: George Edgar Rice.

THOMAS: Mister George Edgar Rice, we should tell you that as of tonight, Hank Daley is no longer with our troupe. He's on his way to Australia.

RICE: Hank Daley is the one I was least interested in among you. Stars. What good are they? They cost money. They cause trouble. No—I want real actors. I want—you.

(They are speechless.)

RICE: And you, young man... *(He goes to* BUCK.*)* I want you for my Prince of Denmark.

(They remain frozen, stunned.)

RICE: Now, you actors, let's get to work!! *(He goes off.)*

(Pause)

EDWARD: What did he say?

JOHN: He wants us to do—

EDWARD: Who is he?

BUCK: Is he—insane?

THOMAS: He can't have the money to—.

*(*RICE *from a distance tosses a bag of gold dust at their feet.)*

RICE: I made a fortune out here selling picks and shovels. Never mined for gold myself—don't like the gamble. I like to bet only on sure things. Like... *(Gestures to them.)* Here. Here is a copy of the play.

*(*RICE *tosses that to them, and goes.)*

(Short pause as they stare at the play.)

ALICE: I've seen this sort of thing happen at the end of a play—but in real life?

JOHN: *(Picking up the bag and the play, to us)* So—we fixed up the stage. Painted it.

EDWARD: *(Taking a part of the play from* JOHN*)* Studied our parts.

*(*EDWARD *passes out the parts.)*

SUSAN: New costumes were made—now especially for us.

THOMAS: We rehearsed.

(A curtain divides the stage and we are suddenly backstage. Music plays and a big cheering, excited audience can be heard through the curtain.)

BUCK: Buck gained confidence by the hour.

(The crowd is getting raucous. We are in the middle of a performance of HAMLET*.)*

*(*ALICE *is alone backstage, she speaks to us as the play continues on the other side of the curtain—we hear only the joy of the audience.)*

ALICE: *(As she gets into her costume)* And so miracle followed miracle. Mister George Edgar Rice was as good as his word. He paid for everything. And to our amazement—the opening was an immediate and extraordinary success.

(From the other side of the curtain: the crowd is cheering.)

ALICE: Word of mouth brought crowds from miles round. Lines snaked down the street. If one can call a mud river with ruts a street. Rumor had it that even the great Booth himself was seen sneaking in for a the last act one matinee.

(First SUSAN, *then* JOHN *enter from "the stage".)*

ALICE: Susan was a beautiful and graceful Ophelia. John, a solid, solicitous Laertes.

(THOMAS *and* RUTH *enter from "the stage".)*

ALICE: Thomas a fine Claudius and Ghost. And Ruth— the Player Queen.

THOMAS: *(Noticing* RUTH's *jewelry)* Where did you get *that* jewelry?

RUTH: I found it in the street.

THOMAS: Next time you go looking for money, I'm going to come with you.

ALICE: Thomas soon moved in with Ruth, leaving Alice all alone—but not for long.

(RICE *enters and approaches* ALICE:)

RICE: *(To* ALICE*)* The ratio of men to women in California at this time being approximately 587 to one, I better take you.

ALICE: *(To* RICE*)* How romantic.

(ALICE *kisses* RICE, *he goes.)*

(SUSAN *giggles at something* JOHN *has said.)*

SUSAN: *(To* JOHN*)* You are so funny.

JOHN: *(Confused)* What? What did I say??

(SUSAN *smiles at* JOHN, *and takes his arm.)*

ALICE: *(To us)* She would get him to propose soon.

(EDWARD *enters from the "wings" with a* MINER.)

EDWARD: A fine Polonius, found a friend as well.

EDWARD: *(To the* MINER*)* Now just sit over there. It's a special seat for guests.

(MINER *feels* EDWARD's *costume.)*

MINER: Nice leather.

(BUCK comes through the curtain from the stage, dressed as Hamlet.)

ALICE: And Buck a wonderful Hamlet. First adored...

(The crowd is cheering for BUCK. He goes out and takes a bow—huge cheer. He returns.)

ALICE: Then...worshipped.

(The crowd is chanting for him. He returns to an even bigger ovation.)

THOMAS: *(To everyone:)* We're on! We're on! Come on!

(They go back "on stage", except for ALICE.)

ALICE: *(To us)* And Alice, of course, was a deeply moving Gertrude.

(THOMAS sticks his head back through the curtain:)

THOMAS: Alice, everyone's on for the end!! *(He goes back "on stage".)*

ALICE: *(To us)* Now you'll have to excuse me, I'm needed. *(She moves to the curtain and is about to go onstage, then stops:)* On second thought, as you've spent all of this time—you'd probably like to see the end of our play. So—come on, come on. It's almost over.

(And as the curtain opens, we are no longer backstage, but in the audience for the play:)

ALICE: Ladies and Gentlemen, The Thomas Jefferson Calhoun Star Troupe's production of—Shakespeare's immortal tragedy—*Hamlet*. As adapted for our times, by George Edgar Rice, with an all new—thank god— happy ending!!

(The stage: BUCK/HAMLET, JOHN/LAERTES lie in agony on the ground after the swordfight. CLAUDIUS stands over them, when EDWARD/OSRIC hurries in:)

OSRIC: There's been a small mistake here, I'll explain— These two right valiant nobles are not slain.

I overheard the most infernal plot
To kill the prince, and swore that they should not;
I had a key made for Laertes' locks,
And searched his bureau till I found the box
That held the poisoned ointment—forced the lid,
Emptied, and put in Russia salve instead.

(HAMLET *and* LAERTES *spring to their feet and embrace*
OSRIC.)

LAERTES: Then we ain't dead—I really did not know,
That from your mouth such pleasant words could flow.

HAMLET: Faith, this is pleasant, Osric, there's my hand.

CLAUDIUS: Lord Hamlet shall be king o'er all the land-

(ALL *shout.*)

HAMLET: Horatio shall be prime minister; my boy
were your gentle sister here, our joy
would be complete.

(HAMLET *slaps* LAERTES *on the back.*)

(SUSAN/OPHELIA *runs in.*)

HAMLET: Is that a phantom there?

OPHELIA: I thought I'd come to see how you all were.

HAMLET: What, ain't you dead?

OPHELIA: I only made believe,
With chloroform.

LAERTES: Why did you so deceive?

OPHELIA: I thought it might bring Hamlet to his senses.

HAMLET:
You rogue, you've made me well by false pretences,—
But now I'm King, and all things shall go right,
We'll have a banquet and a dance to-night,
And if I still am lord of your affection,
Sometime to-morrow, if there's no objection,

We'll have the greatest wedding that's been seen,
In Denmark's land.

OPHELIA: *(Aside)* So I'm to be a queen.
(Aloud) Sir, as this is a time of great hilarity,
I will accept your hand—but out of charity.

HAMLET: I care not, so you'll take it, and my life
Shall be devoted to my charming wife.

(The following is sung to the tune of Oh, Susannah:*)*

OPHELIA: I had a most delightful dream—I think 'twas
Thursday night,
I dreamed, in spite of all my grief, that things would
turn out right;
That Hamlet would come back restored from good old
England's strand,
And I should be his queen and rule with him
throughout the land.

ALL: So, dear ladies, don't you weep for me,
I am very happy now, and soon I'll be a queen, you
see.

HAMLET: That her sweet dream has come to pass is
really quite delightful,
For at one time the aspect of affairs was truly frightful.

But still I thought that soon or late as matters are they
would be,
And Virtue'd be victorious, as Virtue always should
be.

ALL: So, dear public, don't you grieve for me,
I'm kind, and dear Ophelia is to be my queen, you see.
So, dear people, don't just clap for me,
We owe it all to him we call the Bard of the West, you
see!

(And they all gesture to introduce The Bard of the West.)

(Music plays. A banner appears announcing: "George Edgar Rice—The Bard of the West".)

*(*RICE *triumphantly enters dressed as William Shakespeare in chaps, cowboy boots and cowboy hat, waving to the crowd.)*

(Then RICE *holds up his hands to quiet everyone: the music stops.)*

RICE: Ladies and Gentlemen— Can there ever really be—too many—happy endings?!

(Music. RICE *gestures to the wings:)*

(And GEORGE *appears, happy, waving to the crowd—the others gasp, amazed, stunned. They start to go and greet him, but are stopped when* RICE *gestures to the wings again and:)*

*(*HANK *appears, all smiles. a bigger gasp.)*

(And HANK *gestures behind him—and in walks* KATE*! The others are beside themselves now, they go to hug her, when* KATE *stops them, hurries off stage, and returns with—her's and* HANK's *baby in her arms! She lovingly holds up the baby!)*

(The others swoon over the baby, hardly able to believe what has happened. KATE *hands the baby off and the child is passed around to the others to hold.)*

(As they pass the child around, some begin to dance for joy, and so begins a hoe-down, and all dance or play music until:)

END OF PLAY

The following books proved especially useful in researching the play: Helen Wickham Koon's *How Shakespeare Won The West: Players and Performances in America's Gold Rush*; Koon's *Gold Rush Performers: A Biographical Dictionary of Actors, Singers, Dancers, Musicians, Circus Performers and Minstrel Players in America's Far West, 1848-1869*; Arthur Hobson Quinn's *A History of the American Drama, vol I*; *Representative Plays By American Dramatists, vol 2* (edited by Montrose J Moses); Lawrence W Levine's *Highbrow Lowbrow: The Emergence Of Cultural Hierarchy In America*; *Annals Of The New York Stage (various volumes)*; Esther Cloudman Dunn's *Shakespeare In America*; Mary C Henderson's *The City and the Theater: New York Playhouses From Bowling Green to Times Square*; Liza Ketchum's *The Forty-Niners*; Geoffrey C Ward's *The West: An Illustrated History.*

The version of *Hamlet* performed at the end of the play was written by George Edgar Rice and first published in 1852. It is one of the many "travesties" of Shakespeare's plays in the collections of the Shakespeare Institute, Stratford-upon-Avon, England. I am grateful for the Institute's help in researching this play.

The importance of Shakespeare in 19th Century American culture can hardly be overstated, even if it has mostly been forgotten:

"There is hardly a pioneer's hut that does not contain a few odd volumes of Shakespeare. I remember that I read the feudal drama of Henry V for the first time in a log cabin."
—Alexis de Tocqueville, *Democracy In America* (1835)

"There is, assuredly, no other country on earth in which Shakespeare and The Bible are held in such general high esteem as in America."
—Karl Knortz, *Shakespeare In America* (1882)

"A theatrical legend claims that the most popular playwright during the California Gold Rush was William Shakespeare. Improbable as it seems, the legend is true."
—Helen Wickham Koon, *How Shakespeare Won The West: Players and Performances in America's Gold Rush* (1989)